Best Editorial Cartoons of the Year

BEST EDITORIAL CARTOONS OF THE YEAR

1981 EDITION

Edited by
CHARLES BROOKS

Foreword by JAMES J. KILPATRICK

PELICAN PUBLISHING COMPANY
GRETNA 1981

Special acknowledgments are made to the following for permission to use copyrighted material in this volume:

Editorial cartoons by Jeff MacNelly, © Chicago Tribune—New York News Syndicate; Joe Parker, © Turley/Campbell Cartoon Service; Dick Locher, © Chicago Tribune—New York News Syndicate; Al Liederman, © Rothco; Art Henrikson, © Paddock Publications; Ben Wicks, © King Features Syndicate; Ed Valtman, © Rothco; Ed Stein, © NEA; Jim Berry, © NEA; Jimmy Margulies, © Rothco; John Milt Morris, © The Associated Press; Jerry Robinson, © Cartoonists and Writers Syndicate; Frank Interlandi, © Los Angeles Times Syndicate; Hugh Haynie, © Los Angeles Times Syndicate; Lee Judge, © Field Syndicate; Clyde Peterson, © Register and Tribune Syndicate; Dennis Renault, © McClatchy Newspapers; Bill De Ore, © Field Syndicate; Gene Basset, © Scripps Howard Newspapers; John Trever, © Field Syndicate; Don Wright, © The New York Times Syndicate.

Library of Congress Serial Catalog Data

Best editorial cartoons. 1972-
Gretna [La.] Pelican Pub. Co.
v. 29cm. annual-
"A pictorial history of the year."

I. United States- Politics and government—
1969—Caricatures and Cartoons—Periodicals.
E839.5.B45 320.9'7309240207 73-643645
ISSN 0091-2220   MARC-S

Manufactured in the United States of America

Published by Pelican Publishing Company, Inc.
1101 Monroe Street, Gretna, Louisiana 70053

Designed by Barney McKee

Distributed in Canada by Beatty & Church Company Limited

Contents

Foreword

Great editorial cartoonists have this in common with great civilizations: They come along in waves.

When I first became a newspaper editor, charged with producing a daily editorial page, we were in the Dark Ages of cartooning. This was back in 1949. With a couple of exceptions, most of the cartoonists of that day were mediocrities, or worse. For the most part they looked upon the news with neither wit nor understanding. They had few ideas, and these they copied persistently from one another. As Dr. Johnson remarked of some hack's manuscript, the parts that were good were not original, and the parts that were original were not good.

In the time of which I speak, Harry Truman was conducting a running feud with the Congress. Most of the cartoonists could think of but one metaphor, the spanking metaphor. Thus we had Mr. Truman, paddle in hand, hauling Congress out to the woodshed. Or we had Congress coming back from the woodshed, holding the congressional fanny, and you knew the fanny had been spanked because it exuded stars and sizzle marks. In a variation on the theme, Mr. Truman was a schoolmarm, smacking congressional knuckles with a ruler labeled "veto." You knew the knuckles had been smacked because the knuckles exuded sizzle marks and stars.

I tell you, it was a lean time. When the cartoonists were not vending stale metaphors, they were providing tired illustrations: the planet earth as a bomb, with a fuse labeled "Korea," or "Czechoslovakia," or "World Hunger." Some of the boys kept that drawing permanently in stock and pasted in new lettering to suit the occasion. We had the Grim Reaper harvesting death upon the highways. We had the harried taxpayer, his suspenders holding up the inevitable barrel. As late as the middle fifties, Congress was still wearing spats.

And then something happened. The Dark Ages ended and a Renaissance appeared. All of a sudden a whole new breed of editorial cartoonists emerged. They were young men with a glint in their eyes. Their drawing pens dripped blood and acid. They were genuinely, hilariously funny. And miracle of miracles, they could draw—actually draw! Their characters had bones and muscles, and the anatomy was right. Their caricatures were works of art, descended of the same satirical tradition that Rodin brought to his small works of sculpture. And today these

FOREWORD

young Turks are riding high. The state of the cartoonist's art has never been better.

It is a fearfully difficult art, as I may have suggested already. The good editorial writer comes to his typewriter with some rudimentary knowledge of law and politics and government; he ought to know something of economics, literature, and world history; in theory, at least, the good editorial writer has a firm grasp upon the meaning of events. And he has this great advantage: When his wit and erudition fail him, and the editorial writer turns out a poor piece, it is no great embarrassment. The piece simply lies there on the editorial page, a gray anonymity, easily ignored. This is known as laying an egg. I have laid lots of them.

The cartoonist must come to his drawing board with the same education and background, the same general knowledge of history and events, but he has to have much more. He must have the gift of compression—the ability to extract the essence of an idea and to distill it with shutter-speed swiftness into a single drop of critical comment. On top of that, a talent for caricature. And on top of that, the artist's skills of composition, perspective, and draftsmanship. When he lays an egg, everyone knows it! A cartoon hasn't come off. A gag hasn't worked. The idea was stale after all. If a columnist or editorial writer turns out one good piece a week, he's doing acceptably well. If the cartoonist turns out even one bummer a week, he's in trouble.

Presidential election years always are great years for the cartoonists, and 1980 was no exception. The year saw many other events superbly suited for the cartoonist's eye. And as you will see in the following pages, the nation's cartoonists looked upon the passing scene with eyes that were droll, and merry, and sometimes wistful, and sometimes savage. They had one helluva time in 1980, and they proved anew, if proof were required, that one good drawing is worth a thousand words.

JAMES J. KILPATRICK

Award-Winning Cartoons

1980 PULITZER PRIZE

DON WRIGHT
Editorial Cartoonist
Miami News

Born Los Angeles, California, January 23, 1934; award-winning photographer and photo editor; persuaded by editor of *Miami News* to become editorial cartoonist in 1963; Pulitzer Prize, 1966; Sigma Delta Chi Award, 1978; numerous other awards; syndicated by Washington Star Syndicate, 1970-76, New York Times Syndicate, 1976 to present, Newsweek Broadcasting Service, 1978 to present; member of Board of Overseers of Emerson College, Boston.

1980 HEADLINERS CLUB AWARD

1980 OVERSEAS PRESS CLUB AWARD

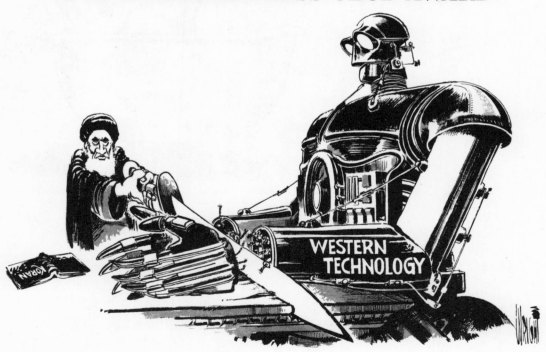

DON WRIGHT
Editorial Cartoonist
Miami News

1979 SIGMA DELTA CHI AWARD
(Selected in 1980)

JOHN TREVER
Editorial Cartoonist
Albuquerque Journal

Born Santa Monica, California, June 13, 1943; graduated from Syracuse University, 1965, magna cum laude in political science, literature, and art; Phi Beta Kappa; graduate study, University of Chicago, 1965-67; staff cartoonist, *Cleveland Plain Dealer,* 1967-68, Sentinel Newspapers, 1972-76, *Albuquerque Journal,* 1976 to present; honored with awards from Suburban Newspaper Association, U.S. Industrial Council, and National Newspaper Association; syndicated by Field Newspaper Syndicate.

1979 NATIONAL NEWSPAPER AWARD / CANADA
(Selected in 1980)

"Just one more time, Pierre."

EDD ULUSCHAK
Editorial Cartoonist
Edmonton Journal

Born North Alberta, Canada, 1944; of Ukrainian-Canadian descent; National Newspaper Award, 1969; twice recipient of Basil Dean Award for outstanding contributions to the field of journalism; many international awards from Germany, Greece, Bulgaria, Japan, Italy, and the United States; editorial cartoonist for the *Edmonton Journal*, 1968 to present.

Best Editorial Cartoons of the Year

JEFF MACNELLY
Richmond News Leader
©Chicago Tribune—New York
News Syndicate

The Reagan Campaign

After three unsuccessful tries for the White House, Ronald Reagan made it in 1980 on the fourth attempt, becoming, at age 69, the oldest man ever elected president. Without question, Reagan brought with him the most conservative philosophy of any president since the 1920s.

Almost from the beginning of the primaries, Reagan held his position as the front-runner. George Bush, John Connally, and others tried in vain to catch him, but never were able to make it a close race. Bush did score a surprising win in the Iowa caucuses in January, but he was unable to maintain his momentum.

In his campaign Reagan hit hard at President Carter's economic policies and their twin offspring, inflation and unemployment. Carter attempted to paint the GOP challenger as a warmonger eager to push the nuclear button. But in their televised debate on October 28 Reagan did a masterful job of defusing the charge, appearing cool, rational, and down to earth.

Reagan won in November by a landslide, taking all but six states and the District of Columbia.

©1980 CHICAGO TRIBUNE

DICK LOCHER
Chicago Tribune
©Chicago Tribune—N.Y.
News Syndicate

CHESTER COMMODORE
Courtesy Chicago Daily Defender

"I'm for the warmonger, and my wife is for the cynical hostage crisis manipulator."

JIM BERRY
©NEA

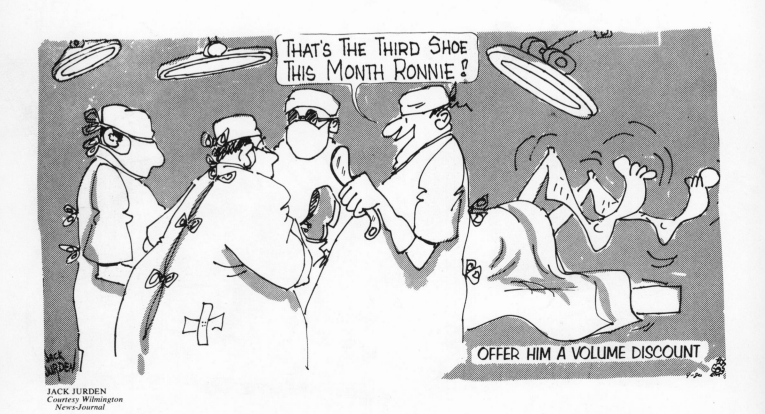

JACK JURDEN
*Courtesy Wilmington
News-Journal*

BOB TAYLOR
Courtesy Dallas Times Herald

STEPHEN SACK
Courtesy Ft. Wayne Journal

JIMMY MARGULIES
©Rothco Cartoons

MARGULIES
ROTHCO

"I'M SUPPORTING REAGAN THIS YEAR BECAUSE HE WANTS TO RETURN THE COUNTRY TO THE WAY THINGS USED TO BE..."

ROBERT GRAYSMITH
Courtesy San Francisco Chronicle

High ~~Drama~~ COMEDY In Detroit

SANDY CAMPBELL
Courtesy The Tennessean

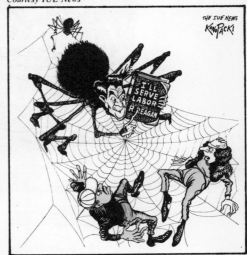

MICHAEL KONOPACKI
Courtesy IUE News

Don't let him fool you,
it's really a cookbook

BOB ENGLEHART
Courtesy Dayton Journal Herald

JERRY FEARING
Courtesy St. Paul Dispatch

STEVE GREENBERG
Courtesy Valley News,
Van Nuys, Cal.

RACE REPORT:
"REAGAN IS STILL LEADING WITH
CARTER JUST A STONE'S THROW BEHIND.
----ANDERSON SEEMS TO BE FADING..."

CHARLES DANIEL
Courtesy Knoxville Journal

The Carter Campaign

Throughout much of the year, President Carter's basic campaign strategy was to stay put in the White House. While others seeking his job were out beating the bushes for votes, Carter remained at his desk, giving as his reason the urgency of his duties.

For several months the strategy appeared to work. But his absence from the campaign trail wore thin with voters, and he felt compelled to venture forth. He pointedly avoided talking about his record in office, attacking Ronald Reagan instead. He painted a portrait of Reagan as a wild-eyed warmonger. The ploy failed, and Carter was widely accused of gutter politics. In the latter stages of the campaign Carter spent much of his time denying that he had a streak of meanness in him.

Carter refused to debate Independent candidate John B. Anderson, concluding that the television exposure could only help his upstart rival. This, too, experts felt, hurt Carter with the voters, who wanted to see the candidates face each other.

GENE BASSET
Courtesy Scripps-Howard Newspapers

"OKAY, HAM... MAKE ME A STAR AGAIN"

Waiting for an October Surprise

JERRY ROBINSON
©Cartoonists and Writers Snydicate

JOHN COLLINS
Courtesy Montreal (Can.) Gazette

"IT'S A QUAINT OLD CUSTOM KNOWN AS ELECTION YEAR"

DOUGLAS BORGSTEDT
Courtesy Philadelphia Daily News

"IT'S DEMOCRATIC PARTY HQ – CAN WE COME UP WITH A DUPLICATE OF F.D.R. BY ELECTION DAY?"

'Maybe There's Something To Be Said
For The Dog Days, After All'

TOM ENGELHARDT
Courtesy St. Louis Post-Dispatch

JOHN CRAWFORD
Courtesy Alabama Journal

TIMOTHY ATSEFF
Syracuse Herald-Journal
©Richmond Syndicate

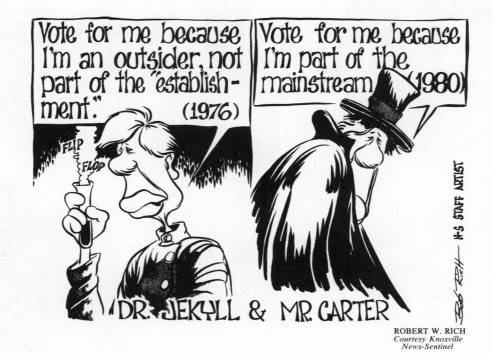

ROBERT W. RICH
*Courtesy Knoxville
News-Sentinel*

DOUG REGALIA
Courtesy Daily Californian

CHESTER COMMODORE
Courtesy Chicago Daily Defender

TWEEDLEDUMB AND TWEEDLEDUMB

"TRUST ME AGAIN, CHARLIE BROWN!"

APOLOGIES TO "PEANUTS"

JIM LANGE
The Daily Oklahoman
©The Oklahoma Publishing Co.

'Khomeini . . . spelled with a K . . . so far I've been voting absentee . . .'

GUERNSEY LEPELLEY
Courtesy Christian Science Monitor

EDDIE GERMANO
Courtesy Brockton Daily Enterprise

ED STEIN
Courtesy Rocky Mountain News

CLYDE PETERSON
Courtesy Houston Chronicle

JACK JURDEN
*Courtesy Wilmington
News-Journal*

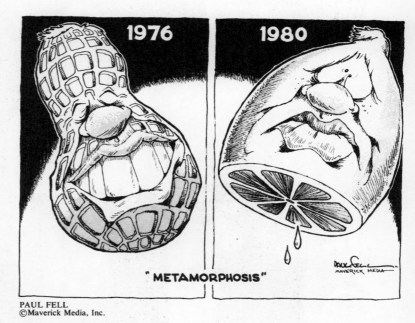

PAUL FELL
©Maverick Media, Inc.

27

DAVID WILEY MILLER
Courtesy Press Democrat,
Santa Rosa, Cal.

JEFF MACNELLY
Richmond News Leader
©Chicago Tribune—New York News Syndicate

28

The Presidential Debates

Under the sponsorship of the League of Women Voters, two presidential debates were held during the campaign of 1980. President Carter refused to take part in any debate in which third-party candidate John B. Anderson participated.

In the first debate—between Ronald Reagan and Anderson—both candidates handled themselves well, but Anderson's candidacy did not get the big lift he had expected. In fact, shortly after the debate with Reagan, Anderson's ratings in the polls began to slip.

The second debate was held in Cleveland on October 28, with Carter facing Reagan. Neither candidate made a major blunder, but Reagan succeeded in "looking presidential," and within a few days it was apparent that the public generally felt Reagan had won. Carter was ridiculed for his assertion that his 13-year-old daughter Amy had advised him that nuclear arms control was the most important issue in the campaign.

BALDY
Courtesy Atlanta Constitution

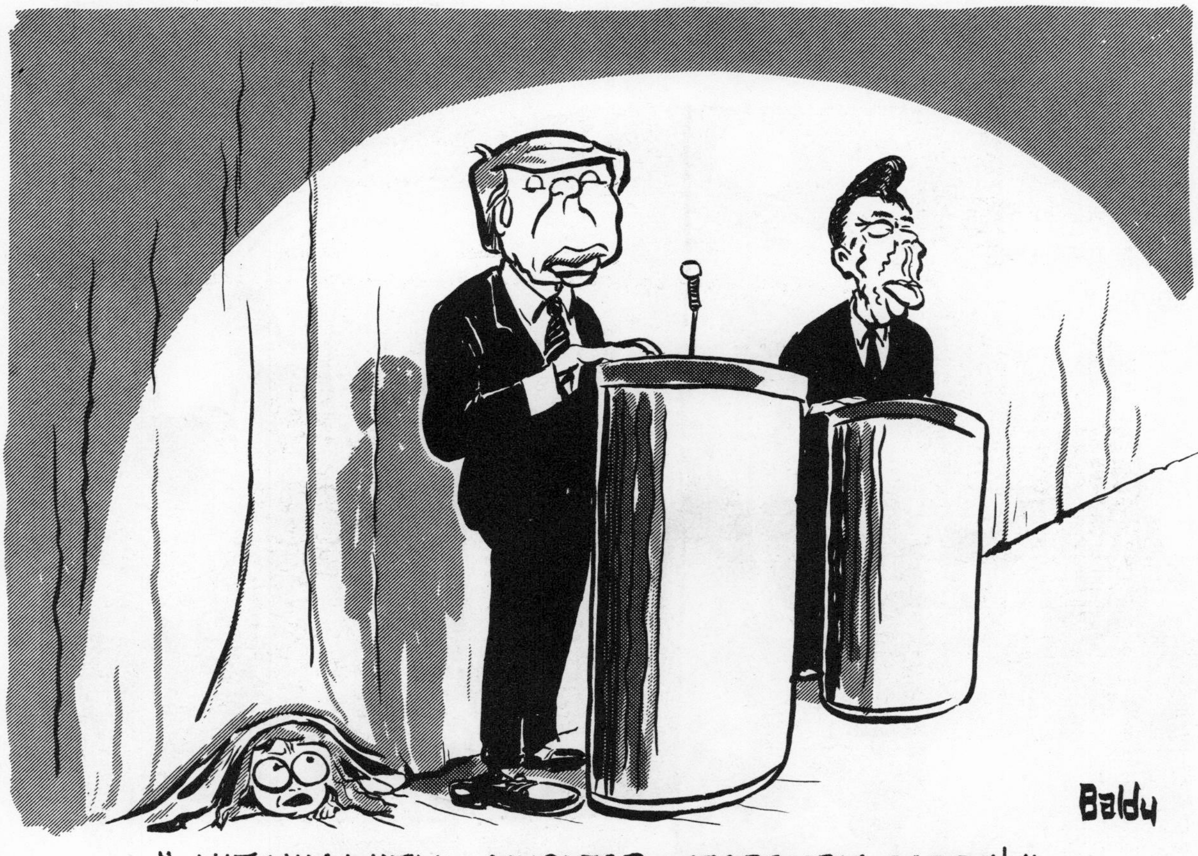
Baldy

"...HIT HIM WITH... NUCLEAR WEAPONRY, DADDY!"

"We have wonderful news Jimmy. Amy has decided to write her memoirs."

JERRY FEARING
Courtesy St. Paul Dispatch

CHUCK AYERS
Courtesy Akron Beacon\Journal

BETTER THAN BILLY OR BERT LANCE!

JIM LANGE
The Daily Oklahoman ©The Oklahoma Publishing Co.

JOHN CRAWFORD
Courtesy Alabama Journal

RAY OSRIN
Courtesy Cleveland Plain Dealer

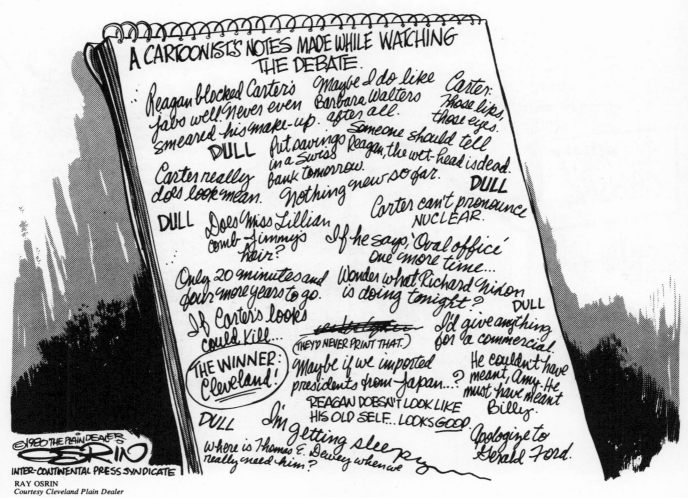

Post-Election Comment

Pollsters declared, even through the final days, that the 1980 presidential election was too close to call. Ronald Reagan had launched his campaign with a huge lead but, according to the polls, President Jimmy Carter had succeeded in closing the gap, and many saw it as a dead heat.

The election was a Reagan landslide and sent pollsters scurrying for explanations. Carter conceded defeat at 9:54 p.m. in the East, long before many polling places had closed on the West Coast. He managed to carry only six states—Georgia, West Virginia, Rhode Island, Minnesota, Maryland, and Hawaii—along with the District of Columbia. Reagan captured the rest, winning 489 electoral votes to 49 for Carter. Independent John Anderson did not win a single state.

It was a humiliating rejection for Carter, who became the first incumbent president to be defeated since Herbert Hoover lost to Franklin D. Roosevelt in 1932.

JOHN FISCHETTI
Courtesy Chicago Sun-Times

BLAINE
Courtesy The Spectator, Canada

JOHN TREVER
Courtesy Albuquerque Journal

33

KEN ALEXANDER
Courtesy San Francisco Examiner

DAVID HORSEY
*Courtesy Seattle
Post-Intelligencer*

HUGH HAYNIE
Louisville Courier-Journal
©Los Angeles Times Syndicate

DRAPER HILL
Courtesy Detroit News

LEW HARSH
Courtesy Scranton Times

DICK WALLMEYER
Long Beach Press-Telegram
©Register and Tribune Syndicate

DEATH VALLEY DAYS

JIM BORGMAN
Courtesy Cincinnati Enquirer

BEDTIME FOR BONZO

RICKY NOBILE
Courtesy Bolivar (Miss.)
Commercial

".FOR SECRETARY OF STATE I'VE CHOSEN A MAN WHO KNOWS HOW TO DEAL WITH THE RUSSIANS...."

TIMOTHY ATSEFF
Syracuse Herald-Journal
©Richmond Syndicate

V. CULLUM ROGERS
Courtesy Durham Morning
Herald

JOHN SHEVCHIK
Courtesy Beaver Falls (Pa.)
News Tribune

DANA SUMMERS
Courtesy Fayetteville
(N. C.) Times

KARL HUBENTHAL
Courtesy Los Angeles
Herald-Examiner

JIM DOBBINS
Courtesy Manchester
Union-Leader

TIM MENEES
Courtesy Pittsburgh
Post-Gazette

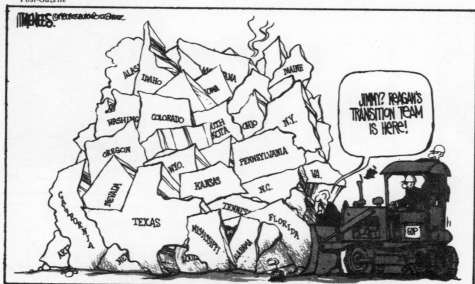

"ME TOO — NOT DOIN' MUCH, JUST HANGIN' AROUND"

JOHN FISCHETTI
Courtesy Chicago Sun-Times

JOHN RIEDELL
Courtesy Peoria Journal

TOM FLANNERY
Courtesy Baltimore Sun

"We're Going to Turn You Around"

BOB GORRELL
Courtesy Charlotte News

TAXIDERMY UNLIMITED

CHARLES BISSELL
Courtesy The Tennessean

ART HENRIKSON
©Paddock Publications

I'm going to see if Mr. Reagan needs a nuclear proliferation adviser!

MERLE TINGLEY
Courtesy London (Can.) Free Press

BOB ZSCHIESCHE
©Bob Zschiesche Syndicate

"YOU CAN RUN BUT YOU CAN'T HIDE!"

HY ROSEN
Courtesy Albany Times-Union

JAMES MORGAN
Courtesy Spartanburg Herald-Journal

JACK BENDER
Waterloo Courier
©Rothco Cartoons, Inc.

DAVID HORSEY
Courtesy Seattle
Post-Intelligencer

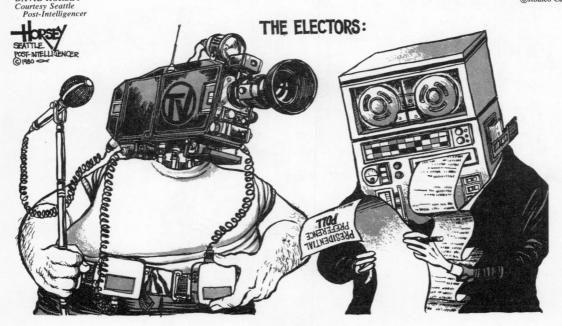

The Carter Administration

In April, the Carter Administration attempted to rescue the American hostages in Iran. Called Operation Eagle Claw, the effort included some 180 handpicked men, about half of them commandos and half aircrew personnel.

The operation was launched on, April 24, with eight helicopters flying to a desert rendezvous with six C-130 transports which had been flown undetected from a base in Egypt. Unexpected problems knocked out three of the helicopters and, with only five still operational, the mission was scrubbed. Eight Americans were killed when one helicopter crashed into one of the C-130s shortly after the decision was made to abort.

All in all, it was not Carter's year. His forecast of a relatively small deficit of $15 billion ballooned to a shortfall of some $60 billion. Unemployment climbed to 7.8 percent and in the automotive industry it exceeded 24 percent. The steel and construction industries also were hard hit. Inflation climbed to 18 percent for a time and averaged 12.5 percent for the year.

Fidel Castro unloaded some 125,000 unwanted Cubans on the U.S. in late April, and Russia continued its efforts to subjugate Afghanistan. More and more Latin America countries were leaning toward Communism. And Carter's dream of a solid Western boycott of the Moscow Olympics failed miserably.

JACK JURDEN
Courtesy Wilmington
News-Journal

BALDY
Courtesy Atlanta Constitution

"...OUR FRIENDS AN' ALLIES ARE **WHERE**? THE HELL YOU SAY!..."

DAVID WILEY MILLER
*Courtesy Press Democrat,
Santa Rosa, Cal.*

'THIS IS NO MORE AS READILY ACCEPTED AS IT USED TO'

ED VALTMAN
©Rothco

DICK LOCHER
Chicago Tribune
©Chicago Tribune—N.Y.
News Syndicate

LEE JUDGE
©Field Syndicate

BERT WHITMAN
Courtesy Phoenix Gazette

JERRY DOYLE
Courtesy Philadelphia Daily News

"...WISH THE OTHER JOINT CHIEFS WOULD HAVE SHOWN UP! PLANNING THIS IRAN RESCUE MISSION HAS DAMMED NEAR GOT ME TUCKERED OUT!"

WHY, AS A MATTER OF FACT, WE ARE LOST. HOW DID YOU KNOW?

"IT'S A LITTLE WEIRD AT FIRST, BUT ZBIGGY AND I HAVE COME TO LIKE IT."

The Moral Majority

During the 1960s, the more liberal churches were generally quick to let their feelings be known about such matters as racial problems and U.S. defense requirements. The conservative churches usually did not publicly declare their stands on issues and, in fact, occasionally protested that politics and religion should not be mixed.

In 1980, however, a new trend began. Many conservatives on the "New Right," which had a strong religious base, began to organize and take an active part in politics on the local and national levels. In many cases they selected slates of candidates whom they backed for various offices.

They maintained the country was turning away from God and that the basic, old-fashioned ideas about morals, sexual behavior, and family structure should be reaffirmed. The leader of the newly formed Moral Majority was the Reverend Jerry Falwell, a television evangelist from Lynchburg, Virginia.

Many such groups sprang up across the country. They targeted ultra-liberals in Congress for defeat and then showed their muscle in helping to turn out of office U.S. senators Frank Church, George McGovern, and Birch Bayh.

GENE BASSET
Courtesy Scripps-Howard Newspapers

"MUST BE ONE OF THOSE MORAL MAJORITY-ITES"

'Does it fire shells or corks?'

JON KENNEDY
Courtesy Arkansas Democrat

JIMMY JOHNSON
Courtesy Jackson (Miss.)
Daily News

"A FEW SUGGESTIONS..."

BA-A-A-A-A-A-A

POLITICAL EXTREMISTS

MORAL MAJORITY

RICHARD CROWSON
Courtesy Jackson (Tenn.) Sun

GEORGE FISHER
Courtesy Arkansas Gazette

49

JOHN FISCHETTI
Courtesy Chicago Sun-Times

THE CREATION

"Thou Shalt Honor the Conservative and Abide Not the Liberal"

TOM FLANNERY
Courtesy Baltimore Sun

The Hostages

The Carter Administration struggled mightily throughout 1980 to gain the release of 52 American hostages being held in Iran, but attempts were repeatedly frustrated. In January, United Nations Secretary-General Kurt Waldheim traveled to Iran on a fact-finding mission, but he was not even allowed to see the hostages or to meet with the Ayatollah Khomeini.

On April 24, U.S. helicopters and jet transports carrying about 180 commandos and support troops attempted to rescue the hostages, but the mission was aborted when the aircraft developed mechanical problems deep in the Iranian interior. Then, in the withdrawal, one of the helicopters collided with a jet on the ground, killing eight U.S. servicemen and injuring nine others.

Shortly before the November election, Iran seemed to be issuing signals that freedom for the hostages was imminent. At year's end the 52 were still being held, but on January 20, 1981, negotiations were concluded and the group was flown to freedom.

PAUL SZEP
Courtesy Boston Globe

'One hundred and eighteen days . . . one hundred and nineteen days . . . one hundred and twenty days . . .'

ROBERT GRAYSMITH
Courtesy San Francisco Chronicle

TIM MENEES
*Courtesy Pittsburgh
Post-Gazette*

BOB ZSCHIESCHE
©Bob Zschiesche Syndicate

Caricatura Nacional
Por BORJA
Tensión

LUIS BORJA
Courtesy La Prensa

JON KENNEDY
Courtesy Arkansas Democrat

"Patience, friend!"

ETTA HULME
Courtesy Ft. Worth Star-Telegram

BRUCE BEATTIE
Courtesy Honolulu Advertiser

"Earl, we got to keep a closer watch on this bird."

DAN BATEY
Courtesy Greenville (Tenn.)
Sun

HAND-HELD WEAPON

VIC CANTONE
Courtesy N.Y. Daily News

54

HUGH HAYNIE
Louisville Courier-Journal
©Los Angeles Times Syndicate

"O'er the land of the free . . . and the home of the hostages."

FRANK INTERLANDI
©Los Angeles Times Syndicate

ENTER THE HOSTAGES – CAMPAIGN '80

DENNIS RENAULT
Courtesy Sacramento Bee

The Sacramento Bee

"HOW DO I SPELL 'RELEASE'? K-H-O-M-E-I-N-I."

CHARLES BROOKS
Courtesy Birmingham (Ala.) News

55

DICK WRIGHT
*Courtesy Providence
Journal-Bulletin*

CLYDE PETERSON
Courtesy Houston Chronicle

'Try as I might, I can't seem to put the hostage crisis behind me'

'How Many Times Must I Count to Ten?'

JOHN STAMPONE
Courtesy Army Times

56

JOE PARKER
©Turley/Campbell Cartoon
Service

CHUCK ASAY
*Courtesy Colorado Springs
Sun*

Iran

Iran made faltering efforts to stabilize its government in 1980, with the Revolutionary Council yielding some of its authority to a president who was elected in January. A parliament was installed in May, and a prime minister and cabinet were named in September. Ayatollah Khomeini, however, remained the nation's supreme leader.

Iranians stuck to their demands that the former Shah be returned to them for trial right up until the moment of his death on July 27. Even after he died, Iranian leaders continued to insist that the U.S. return his wealth.

In the wake of protracted threats, charges, and countercharges, open warfare broke out between Iran and Iraq in September, with each country heavily damaging the oil production capabilities of the other. As the year ended, the war continued, with both sides suffering heavy human and economic losses.

ED ASHLEY
Courtesy Toledo Blade

M. G. LORD
Courtesy Newsday

TOM ENGELHARDT
Courtesy St. Louis Post-Dispatch

'Governments Have Different Departments Or Ministries,
But In Iran...'

STEPHEN SACK
Courtesy Ft. Wayne Journal

DICK WALLMEYER
Long Beach Press-Telegram
©Register and Tribune Syndicate

BOB TAYLOR
Courtesy Dallas Times Herald

ROY PETERSON
Courtesy Vancouver Sun

Releasing the Hostages

ANDY DONATO
Courtesy Toronto Sun

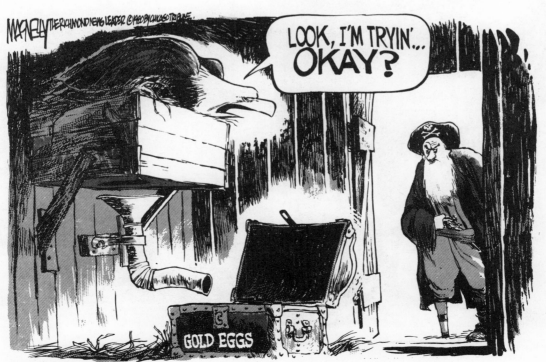

LOOK, I'M TRYIN'... OKAY?

GOLD EGGS

JEFF MACNELLY
Richmond News Leader
©Chicago Tribune—New York
News Syndicate

61

PATRICK CROWLEY
*Courtesy West Palm Beach
Post*

ED GAMBLE
*Courtesy Florida
Times-Union*

ANTHONY JENKINS
Courtesy Toronto Globe and Mail

JOHN R. THORNTON
*Courtesy Republican Journal
(Belfast, Me.)*

LEW HARSH
Courtesy Scranton Times

ROB LAWLOR
Courtesy Philadelphia Daily News

CLYDE PETERSON
Courtesy Houston Chronicle

BOB GORRELL
Courtesy Charlotte News

"I DON'T THINK "T.R." WOULD LIKE THE BIG STICK POLICY TODAY."

JIM DOBBINS
*Courtesy Manchester
Union-Leader*

64

PERSIAN RUG

JOHN RIEDELL
Courtesy Peoria Journal

BERT WHITMAN
Courtesy Phoenix Gazette

RICHARD ALLISON
Courtesy St. Joseph (Mo.)
Gazette

MARGULIES
ROTHCO

"... NOW THREE SOMERSAULTS, FIVE CARTWHEELS AND TWO HANDSPRINGS, THEN A BACK FLIP, AND A PIROUETTE FOLLOWED BY TWO CARTWHEELS..."

DANI AGUILA
Courtesy Filipino Reporter

John Anderson

John B. Anderson, ten-term United States congressman from Illinois, decided to seek the presidency as an Independent after he was unable to beat front-runner Ronald Reagan for the Republican nomination in the primaries. Anderson, a persuasive speaker, issued a strong appeal to liberals and young voters. Polls consistently showing a large number of undecided voters led him to believe he might pick up a sizable following.

In mid-June, a Gallup poll gave 23 percent of the vote to Anderson, but by August his share had dropped to 15 percent. His popularity continued to slide, even after he appeared in a nationally televised debate with Reagan on September 13, a confrontation he had diligently sought.

In the final balloting, he won only 7 percent of the popular vote and no electoral votes. His showing was respectable for a third-party candidate, however, and qualified him for federal campaign funds. His vote total also qualified him for partial federal funding in 1984 in the event he decides to run again.

KARL HUBENTHAL
Courtesy Los Angeles
Herald-Examiner

"WILL THIS STRANGE ANIMAL SURVIVE IN THIS ENVIRONMENT"

KEN ALEXANDER
Courtesy San Francisco Examiner

RICHARD ALLISON
Courtesy St. Joseph (Mo.) Gazette

ED FISCHER
Courtesy Omaha World-Herald

JERRY BARNETT
Courtesy Indianapolis News

FRANK EVERS
Courtesy N. Y. Daily News

JOHN TREVER
Courtesy Albuquerque Journal

Ted Kennedy

In late 1979, the Democratic nomination for president seemed to be Senator Edward Kennedy's for the asking because of President Carter's dismal standing in most political polls. So, on November 7, 1979, Kennedy announced his candidacy. At the time, he led Carter by a two-to-one margin in the polls.

But for a variety of reasons—the hostage issue, the Russian invasion of Afghanistan, and many people's perception of Senator Kennedy's personal character—voters began to turn back to the incumbent president. The swing was swift and dramatic, and Kennedy's lead quickly evaporated.

A CBS interview in late 1979 was a disaster for Kennedy. He was fuzzy on the issues and displayed a poor understanding of what voters perceived to be vital matters.

According to several polls, Chappaquiddick still played a major role in creating voter suspicion of Kennedy. About one-third of those who said they would vote against him reported doubts about his integrity and his stability in a crisis.

Kennedy nevertheless appeared at the Democratic Convention and called for fidelity to the cause of "old-fashioned liberalism." And, despite crushing setbacks, he seemed to have his eye on 1984.

ETTA HULME
Courtesy Ft. Worth Star-Telegram

"I'm afraid the bouef bourguignonne *may have been your Chappaquiddick.*"

JIM BERRY
©NEA

"OK Jimmy, You've Proved Your Point"

EDDIE GERMANO
Courtesy Brockton Daily Enterprise

The Boston Globe

PAUL SZEP
Courtesy Boston Globe

"Hope you'll be able to make it to my nomination, Teddy!"

CHARLES DANIEL
Courtesy Knoxville Journal

BILL GRAHAM
Courtesy Arkansas Gazette

END OF THE TRAIL

JOHN FISCHETTI
Courtesy Chicago Sun-Times

The Middle East

President Carter was pelted with criticism both from his fellow country-men and from Israel when, on March 1, the U.S. voted for a strongly worded United Nations resolution condemning Israeli settlements in the occupied West Bank and the Gaza Strip. Two days later, Carter claimed a "communications failure" had led to the vote, which he insisted had not been intended. His announcement created an even greater furor, along with a growing number of charges that the administration was simply inept.

Egypt and Israel continued to be mired in their efforts to implement the 1978 Camp David Accord. The target date for a successful end to negotiations for Palestinian autonomy in Gaza and the West Bank passed with no agreement in sight.

On September 17 war erupted between Iraq and Iran. Each side inflicted heavy damage on the facilities of the other's vast oil industry, and other OPEC nations agreed to increase their oil shipments to offset the loss of oil from the warring countries.

The Soviet Union continued its efforts to subdue inadequately armed Afghanistan, while the Afghans maintained a dogged resistance. As the year ended, the Soviets stepped up their use of saturation bombing and used napalm and antipersonnel weapons against their ill-equipped foe.

WEST BANK TALKS

ROBERT GRAYSMITH
Courtesy San Francisco Chronicle

SO COMFORTING TO KNOW WE HAVE ONE!

JOHN MILT MORRIS
©The Associated Press

CHARLES BROOKS
Courtesy Birmingham (Ala.) News

"Look at Our MIGs Zap Their Shermans!"

TOM FLANNERY
Courtesy Baltimore Sun

76

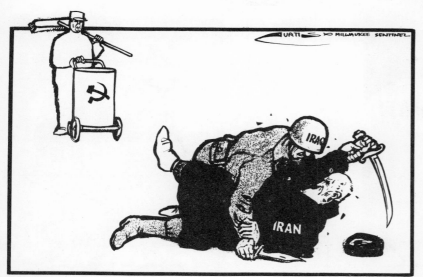

TOM CURTIS
Courtesy Milwaukee Sentinel

'It's a gift . . . never mind the price tag'

GUERNSEY LEPELLEY
Courtesy Christian Science Monitor

MIKE KEEFE
Courtesy Denver Post

PAUL FELL
©Maverick Media, Inc.

DENNIS RENAULT
Courtesy Sacramento Bee

DANA SUMMERS
*Courtesy Fayetteville
(N. C.) Times*

BILL GARNER
Courtesy The Commercial Appeal

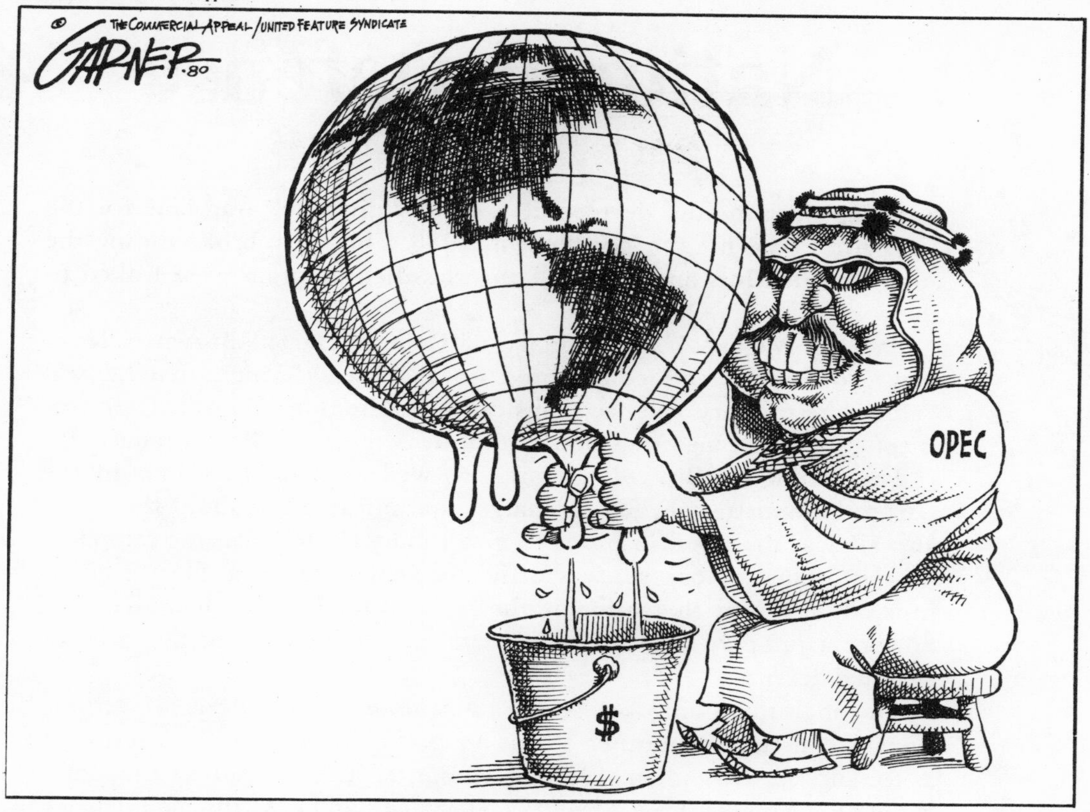
© THE COMMERCIAL APPEAL/UNITED FEATURE SYNDICATE
GARNER ·80
OPEC
$

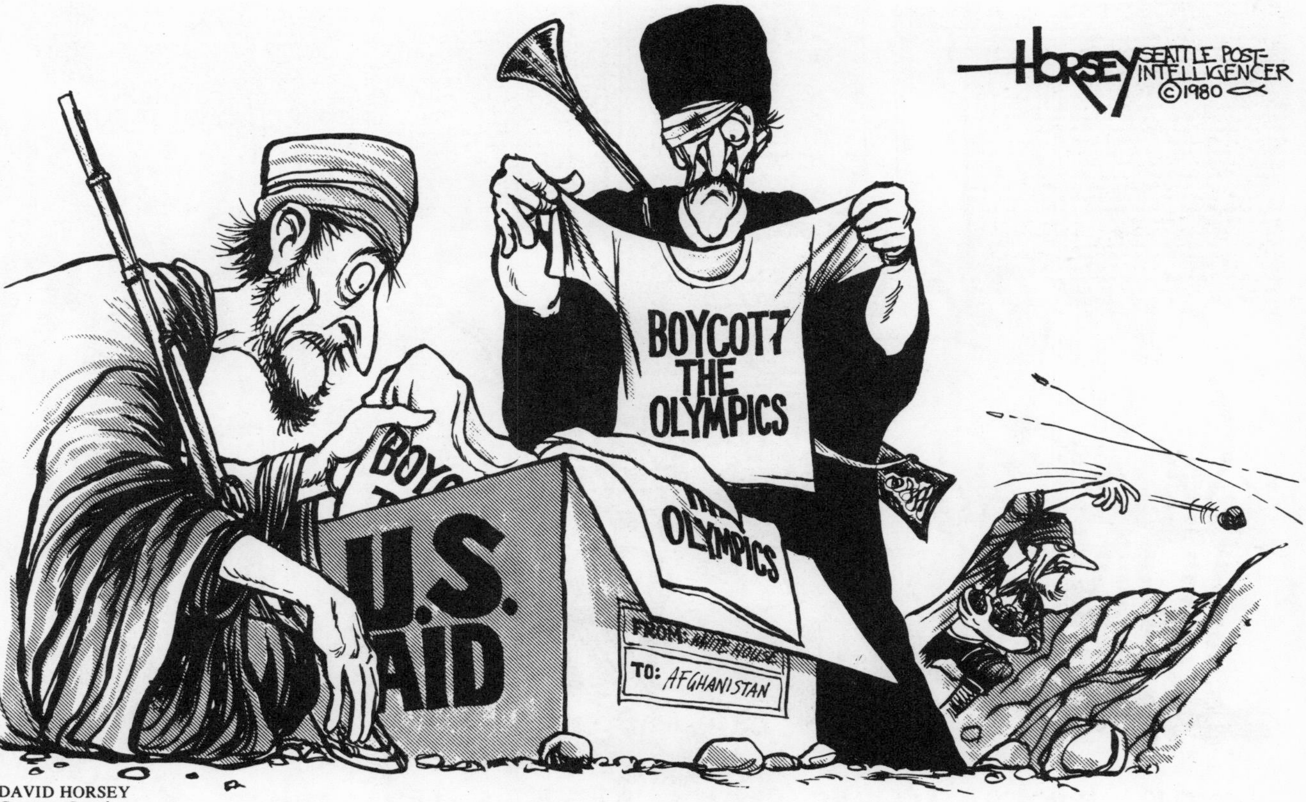
HORSEY SEATTLE POST-INTELLIGENCER ©1980
BOYCOTT THE OLYMPICS
BOYC
U.S. AID
THE OLYMPICS
FROM: WHITE HOUSE
TO: AFGHANISTAN

DAVID HORSEY
Courtesy Seattle Post-Intelligencer

National Defense

Startling news of the development of an "invisible" warplane for the U.S. Air Force hit the headlines in 1980. The story broke during the summer when bits and pieces of the classified program were leaked to the press.

Late in August, U.S. Secretary of Defense Harold Brown called a news conference and commented on the breakthrough that he said "alters the military balance significantly." The bomber, called *Stealth*, is constructed of materials that cannot be detected by Soviet radar.

The timing of Brown's remarks, as well as those of others in the Carter Administration, led to charges that information about the secret aircraft was disclosed in order to give Jimmy Carter's sagging campaign a boost. This, of course, was officially denied. Many military sources insisted, however, that bringing the secret into the open had given the Soviets a jump of three to five years in this highly sensitive area of national defense.

The malfunctioning of America's outdated computerized warning system constituted another threat to national security. As a result of a foul-up in November 1979, a computer transmitted a war-games simulation tape as if an actual Soviet attack had been launched. During 1980, the system repeatedly blurted out erroneous information that hostile missile strikes were being made.

DRAPER HILL
Courtesy Detroit News

JOHN CRAWFORD
Courtesy Alabama Journal

BRIAN BASSET
Courtesy Seattle Times

ED ASHLEY
Courtesy Toledo Blade

PATRICK CROWLEY
*Courtesy West Palm Beach
  Post*

LARRY WRIGHT
Courtesy Detroit News

GARY HUCK
Courtesy Racine (Wisc.) Labor

Registered Male

ELDON PLETCHER
New Orleans Times-Picayune
©Rothco

JERRY BARNETT
Courtesy Indianapolis News

BRUCE PLANTE
Courtesy Arkansas Democrat

ETTA HULME
Courtesy Ft. Worth Star-Telegram

TERRY MOSHER (AISLIN)
Courtesy Montreal Gazette

DAN ADAMS
Courtesy Hillsboro, Ore.,
Argus

TITAN II WARNING SYSTEM

BRUCE PLANTE
Courtesy Arkansas Democrat

JOHN STAMPONE
Courtesy Army Times

CHARLES BISSELL
Courtesy The Tennessean

"We've Given The World Another Gray Hair. . .Tired Old
Nukes That Blow Themselves Up!"

JIM PALMER
*Courtesy Montgomery
Advertiser*

The U.S. Economy

Inflation and recession took turns punching the U.S. economy into a state of grogginess during the year. More than 800,000 workers in the automobile and related manufacturing industries were laid off as the economy slowed to a crawl.

For the first quarter, the Consumer Price Index shot up at an annual rate of more than 18 percent. Financing for housing was undermined by the Federal Reserve Board's tight money policies, which were aimed at fighting inflation. The rate of inflation wound up at 12.5 percent for the year.

It was actually a blue-collar recession, with unemployment highest among union workers. Japanese-made automobiles made big gains in 1980, at the expense of American-made products, because of their better gas mileage and a general perception that they were of higher quality.

The government stepped in and bailed out Chrysler to the tune of 1.5 billion in order to keep the company from going bankrupt. At year's end, it was still not clear whether the giant automaker would survive.

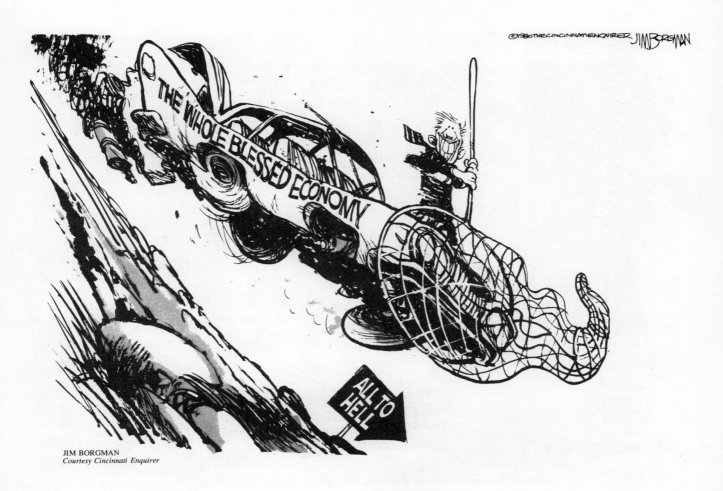

JIM BORGMAN
Courtesy Cincinnati Enquirer

DICK WRIGHT
*Courtesy Providence
Journal-Bulletin*

DICK LOCHER
Chicago Tribune
©Chicago Tribune—N.Y.
News Syndicate

CLYDE WELLS
Courtesy Augusta (Ga.) Chronicle

TOM ENGELHARDT
Courtesy St. Louis Post-Dispatch

'There's Only One Economic Indicator I Go By'

RICHARD ALLISON
Courtesy St. Joseph (Mo.)
Gazette

JERRY FEARING
Courtesy St. Paul Dispatch

MERLE TINGLEY
Courtesy London (Can.) Free Press

"Oh, This is Terrible! Next Year the Price of Automobiles Will be Going Up!"

ALBERTO HUICI
Courtesy Jueves de Excelsior (Mex.)

BIG JOB FOR A LITTLE FELLA!

JOHN MILT MORRIS
©The Associated Press

ED ASHLEY
Courtesy Toledo Blade

90

DEORE
The Dallas Morning News. Field Syndicate 1980

BILL DE ORE
Courtesy Dallas Morning News

JAPAN

U.S. FORD

U.S. CHRYSLER

GENE BASSET
Courtesy Scripps-Howard Newspapers

TORA, TORA, TORA

BOB ZSCHIESCHE
©Bob Zschiesche Syndicate

LEANING TOWER

ART WOOD
Courtesy Farm Bureau News

ED GAMBLE
Courtesy Florida Times-Union

CHUCK AYERS
Courtesy Akron Beacon Journal

LARRY WRIGHT
Courtesy Detroit News

RAY OSRIN
Courtesy Cleveland Plain Dealer

"COOL IT!"

ART WOOD
Courtesy Farm Bureau News

CLYDE PETERSON
Courtesy Houston Chronicle

THE L. A. TIMES SYNDICATE

HUGH HAYNIE
Louisville Courier-Journal
©Los Angeles Times Syndicate

94

Inflation

During the first quarter of 1980, inflation surged upward at the staggering rate of 18.1 percent, but as the year wore on it slackened, ending with a 12.5 percent mark overall for 1980.

The Federal Reserve Board policy of increasing interest rates to combat inflation caused home mortgage payments to soar. Mortgage interest rates climbed to as high as 17 percent in early spring, but by midsummer had dropped to the 12 to 13 percent range.

The first half of the year saw a decline in productivity. Some economists began comparing the U.S. economic plight with that of Great Britain when it started its long slide from economic preeminence more than a decade ago. America's aging manufacturing base was becoming more and more threatened by intense foreign competition.

ED GAMBLE
Courtesy Florida Times-Union

"SURE, WE MIGHT BE ABLE TO HAVE ONE SOMEDAY.....IF THE GOVERNMENT WILLS IT, SON!"

ED ASHLEY
Courtesy Toledo Blade

EDD ULUSCHAK
Courtesy Edmonton Journal

"Good news — our credit check shows you can't afford any serious ailments."

ED STEIN
*Courtesy Rocky Mountain
News*

96

STEPHEN SACK
Courtesy Ft. Wayne Journal

JOHN KNUDSEN
Courtesy N.Y. Catholic News

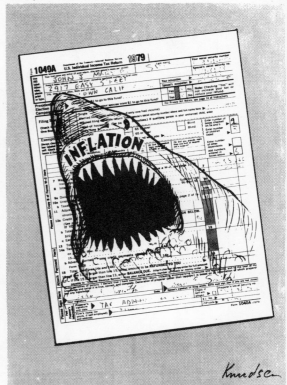

The bite is bigger this year

PAUL SZEP
Courtesy Boston Globe

"The Nation Has Turned The Corner On Inflation —

LARRY WRIGHT
Courtesy Detroit News

JACK BENDER
Waterloo Courier
©Rothco Cartoons, Inc.

EUGENE CRAIG
Courtesy Columbus (O.) Dispatch

Energy

Energy problems and related matters continued to dominate the news throughout 1980. In September, the OPEC nations agreed to reduce their crude oil output by 10 percent and raise prices at the same time. After war flared up between Iraq and Iran, Saudi Arabia and other OPEC countries increased their production to compensate for the loss of oil from the two warring Arab nations.

American coal production continued to increase in 1980, reaching about 3.9 billion tons, roughly 5 percent more than in 1979.

Gasohol, a blend of 90-percent gasoline and 10-percent ethyl alcohol, was seen as a growing alternative on the American market. The Carter Administration launched a program that was intended to provide between $8.5 billion and $13 billion in federal assistance to stimulate production of alcohol fuels over the coming decade.

On June 29, decontamination of the crippled Three Mile Island nuclear reactor near Middletown, Pennsylvania, was begun. Engineers entered the building in July for the first time since a major accident in 1979. The cleanup is expected to take several years and will cost about $1 billion.

TIM MENEES
Courtesy Pittsburgh Post-Gazette

BOB ALEXANDER
Courtesy Lawrence (Mass.) Eagle-Tribune

BOB SULLIVAN
Courtesy Worcester (Mass.) Telegram

VIC RUNTZ
Courtesy Bangor Daily News

JACK McLEOD
Courtesy Buffalo Evening News

BLAINE
Courtesy The Spectator, Canada

"It's All Right — He's One of Us!"

ELDON PLETCHER
New Orleans Times-Picayune
©Rothco

VIC CANTONE
Courtesy N.Y. Daily News

The Environment

The top environmental issue of the year was the handling of hazardous chemical wastes. On July 22, a container holding nearly 13 tons of a deadly poison fell overboard when ships collided in a man-made passage between the Mississippi River and the Gulf of Mexico. About 400 miles of fishing grounds and oyster beds were closed for a brief period.

Canisters filled with deadly chemicals sank in the English Channel near the end of 1979, causing great concern. Explosions and a fire at a closed chemical plant in Elizabeth, New Jersey, in April caused more problems, and residents were advised to avoid breathing the smoke.

The Environmental Protection Agency began phasing in strict regulations on the handling and disposal of hazardous wastes in accordance with the Resource Conservation and Recovery Act of 1976. The public seemed to demand that more be done to stop the irresponsible disposal of hazardous materials.

JOHN TREVER
Courtesy Albuquerque Journal

"WE'RE BEING SUED BY THE NATIONAL ASSOCIATION OF MANUFACTURERS. THEY SAY THE EMISSIONS FROM OUR MOUNTAINS ARE SPOILING THE AIR OVER THEIR FACTORIES!"

"MOUNT ST. HELENS, I HEREBY ARREST YOU IN THE NAME OF THE UNITED STATES GOVERNMENT AND ENVIRONMENTALISTS EVERYWHERE FOR POLLUTING!"

CHARLES BROOKS
Courtesy Birmingham (Ala.) News

PRESIDENT VISITS MOUNT ST. HELENS

JIM LANGE
The Daily Oklahoman
©The Oklahoma Publishing Co.

STEPHEN SACK
Courtesy Ft. Wayne Journal

"NOW BEHAVE YOURSELF...."

PAUL DUGINSKI
Courtesy Sacramento Union

'I suppose the media will make a big deal out of this'

CRAIG MACINTOSH
Courtesy Minneapolis Star

MIKE KEEFE
Courtesy Denver Post

BOB SULLIVAN
Courtesy Worcester (Mass.) Telegram

"Here is the news. During the night the world was destroyed by chemical waste leaving just two survivors."

BEN WICKS
©King Features

BOB ALEXANDER,
*Courtesy Eagle-Tribune,
Lawrence, Mass.*

Women's Rights

For the third year in a row, the number of states ratifying the Equal Rights Amendment remained unchanged at thirty-five. To become law, the measure requires ratification by three more states by June 30, 1982.

Clouding the issue, however, have been the repeal by several states of their previous ratifications and the controversial extension of the ratification deadline by Congress.

The Democratic Party endorsed the ERA in its platform during the 1980 presidential campaign; the Republican Party platform did not endorse the ERA. The GOP, however, did express strong support for equal rights for women.

"BE CAREFUL, PENDLETON. YOU CAN STILL BE BURNED AS A WITCH."

'You go on ahead to the ERA rally, Evie, this may take some time'

CRAIG MACINTOSH
Courtesy Minneapolis Star

CHUCK ASAY
Courtesy Colorado Springs Sun

DENNIS RENAULT
Courtesy Sacramento Bee

109

FRANK INTERLANDI
©Los Angeles Times Syndicate

ED FISCHER
Courtesy Omaha World-Herald

BOB ARTLEY
Courtesy Worthington (Minn.) Daily Globe

After much huffing and puffing and pulling and shoving . . .

U.S. Congress

The FBI's elaborate Abscam operation had a far-reaching impact on the U.S. Congress during 1980. Federal agents posing as middlemen for oil-rich Arab sheiks offered congressmen money to introduce and support special-interest legislation.

By fall, some two dozen individuals, including six members of the House of Representatives and one U.S. senator, had been indicted. Congressman Michael Myers, a Democrat from Pennsylvania, was found guilty of accepting a $50,000 bribe. Other convictions seemed likely.

The state of the economy held the attention of the lawmakers throughout the year as unemployment continued to spread. As the recession worsened, Congress realized it could not balance the 1981 budget. It did, however, deregulate the trucking and railroad industries, a move that had the support of the administration.

FRANK EVERS
Courtesy N. Y. Daily News

JERRY DOYLE
Courtesy Philadelphia Daily News

DRAPER HILL
Courtesy Detroit News

COATTAILS

VERN THOMPSON
Courtesy Lawton (Okla.) Constitution

BILL DE ORE
Courtesy Dallas Morning News

CONGRESSMAN

CON...SMAN

"If you go to jail we may have to censure you."

BRUCE BEATTIE
Courtesy Honolulu Advertiser

JIM ORTON
©Computer World

ROBERT W. RICH
*Courtesy Knoxville
News-Sentinel*

'Not bad — except for a couple of issues where the other side of his mouth is still silent.'

"HOUSE CLEANING"

He Didn't Say, "BUY The People"

REG·MANNING
REG MANNING
Courtesy Arizona Republic

DRAPER HILL
Courtesy Detroit News

ED VALTMAN
©Rothco

'SORRY, IT WAS ONE OF THOSE UNNECESSARY OPERATIONS. BUT I WANT YOU TO KNOW I KEEP MY FINGERS CROSSED FOR YOUR SPEEDY RECOVERY'

BOB ENGLEHART
Courtesy Dayton Journal Herald

" I HAVE NO PROBLEM WITH RELIGION IN POLITICS. I NEED TO EXPLOIT ALL THE GROUPS I CAN! "

Canadian Politics

The long, simmering squabble between Ottawa and Quebec subsided temporarily when the province's voters rejected a proposal in May that called for political independence from Canada.

Canada's national pride was stirred on January 27 when its ambassador to Iran, Kenneth Taylor, and his staff dramatically rescued six U.S. diplomats from the heart of Iran. The six had escaped from the U.S. embassy compound in Tehran during the takeover by Iranian militants on November 4. The Americans were hidden and sheltered by the Canadians and later smuggled out of the country under Canadian passports.

In February, Pierre Elliott Trudeau and his Liberal Party won a sweeping victory, ousting Prime Minister Joe Clark and the Progressive Conservatives. Clark and his party had been in power only nine months.

Canada's economy took a turn for the worse when America's economic fortunes began to sag. American-owned companies dominate Canadian industry, and the new government announced its intention to change things. A growing nationalism has led to various steps being taken to assist Canadian companies in buying out American-owned firms.

BOB SULLIVAN
Courtesy Worcester Telegram

ANDY DONATO
Courtesy Toronto Sun

JOHN COLLINS
Courtesy Montreal (Can.) Gazette

Ring Around the Referendum

ROY PETERSON
Courtesy Vancouver Sun

THE PQ MONSTER

JOHN COLLINS
Courtesy Montreal (Can.) Gazette

JACK McLEOD
Courtesy Buffalo Evening News

TERRY MOSHER (AISLIN)
Courtesy Montreal Gazette

FAIRY STORY

ANTHONY JENKINS
Courtesy Toronto Globe and Mail

Trudeau: "President Portillo, We Have a Petroleum Problem. . ."

RAOUL HUNTER
Courtesy Le Soleil (Quebec)

MERLE TINGLEY
Courtesy London (Can.) Free Press

EDD ULUSCHAK
Courtesy Edmonton Journal

"Think I've got a bite!"

The Soviet Union

The Russian invasion of Afghanistan, which was launched in late 1979, continued through 1980. The Soviets poured more manpower and materiel into the country, and by late summer it was apparent they were digging in for a long stay. They began construction of air bases, barracks, fuel depots, roads, bridges, and even an oil pipeline.

The interlopers were met with continuous resistance in the mountains and villages throughout the country. It was said that the Afghans will tolerate poverty and insecurity—but not foreign rule. The actions of the determined guerrilla bands operating across Afghanistan seemed to bear this out.

The Soviet Union experienced a severe crop failure in 1979 and had hoped for a better year in 1980. But, because of poor weather and Soviet agricultural mismanagement, the yield was again low. To ease the effect of the U.S. grain embargo, Russia signed a long-term agreement with Argentina to buy more than 22 million tons of corn, soybeans, and sorghum at premium prices. Even these imports were not regarded as enough to fill the Russian breadbasket, however.

Throughout the year the Soviets continued to build up their military forces. In this important area there was no slackening at all.

'ANY OUTSIDE INTERFERENCE WILL NOT BE TOLERATED'

ED VALTMAN
©Rothco

121

JAMES LARRICK
Courtesy Clarion-Ledger,
Jackson, Miss.

VERN THOMPSON
Courtesy Lawton (Okla.) Constitution

DAN ADAMS
Courtesy Hillsboro, Ore.,
Argus

KEN ALEXANDER
Courtesy San Francisco Examiner

EDD ULUSCHAK
Courtesy Edmonton Journal

ROY PETERSON
Courtesy Vancouver Sun

"Too many strings, comrade . . . too many strings . . . ."

JERRY ROBINSON
©Cartoonists and Writers
Snydicate

DAVE GRANLUND
Courtesy Middlesex News

ED GAMBLE
*Courtesy Florida
Times-Union*

124

DANA SUMMERS
*Courtesy Fayetteville
(N. C.) Times*

VERN THOMPSON
Courtesy Lawton (Okla.) Constitution

TOM CURTIS
Courtesy Milwaukee Sentinel

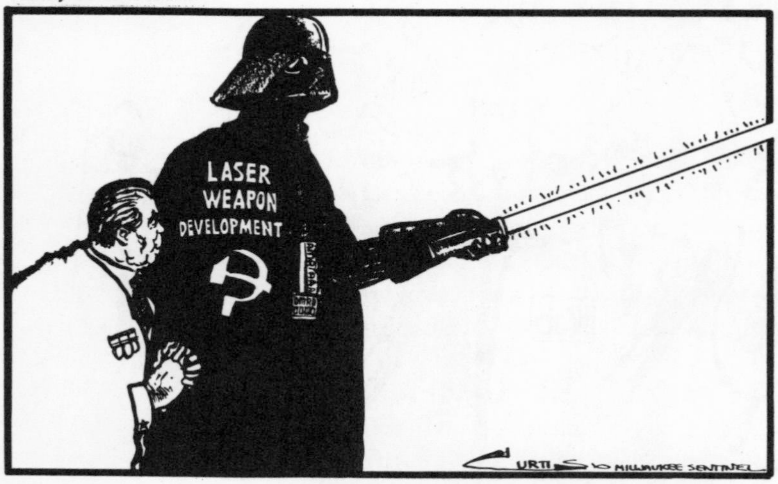
LASER
WEAPON
DEVELOPMENT
CURTIS MILWAUKEE SENTINEL

"The force be with you!"

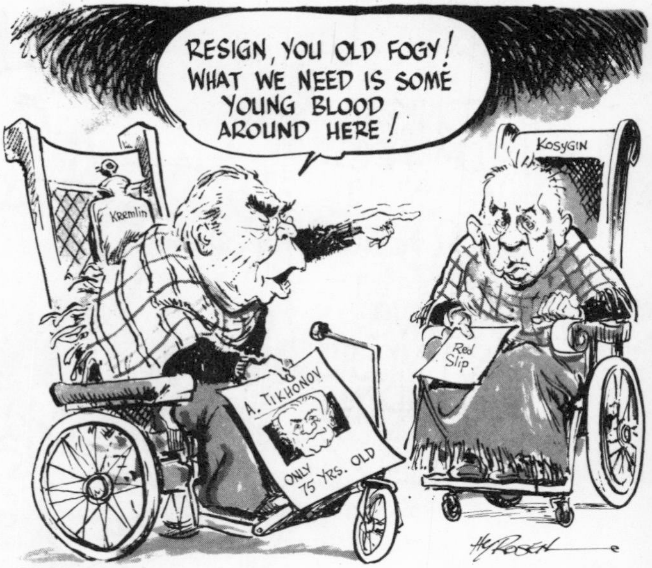
RESIGN, YOU OLD FOGY! WHAT WE NEED IS SOME YOUNG BLOOD AROUND HERE!
Kremlin
KOSYGIN
A. TIKHONOV
ONLY 75 YRS. OLD
Red Slip.
HY ROSEN

HY ROSEN
Courtesy Albany Times-Union

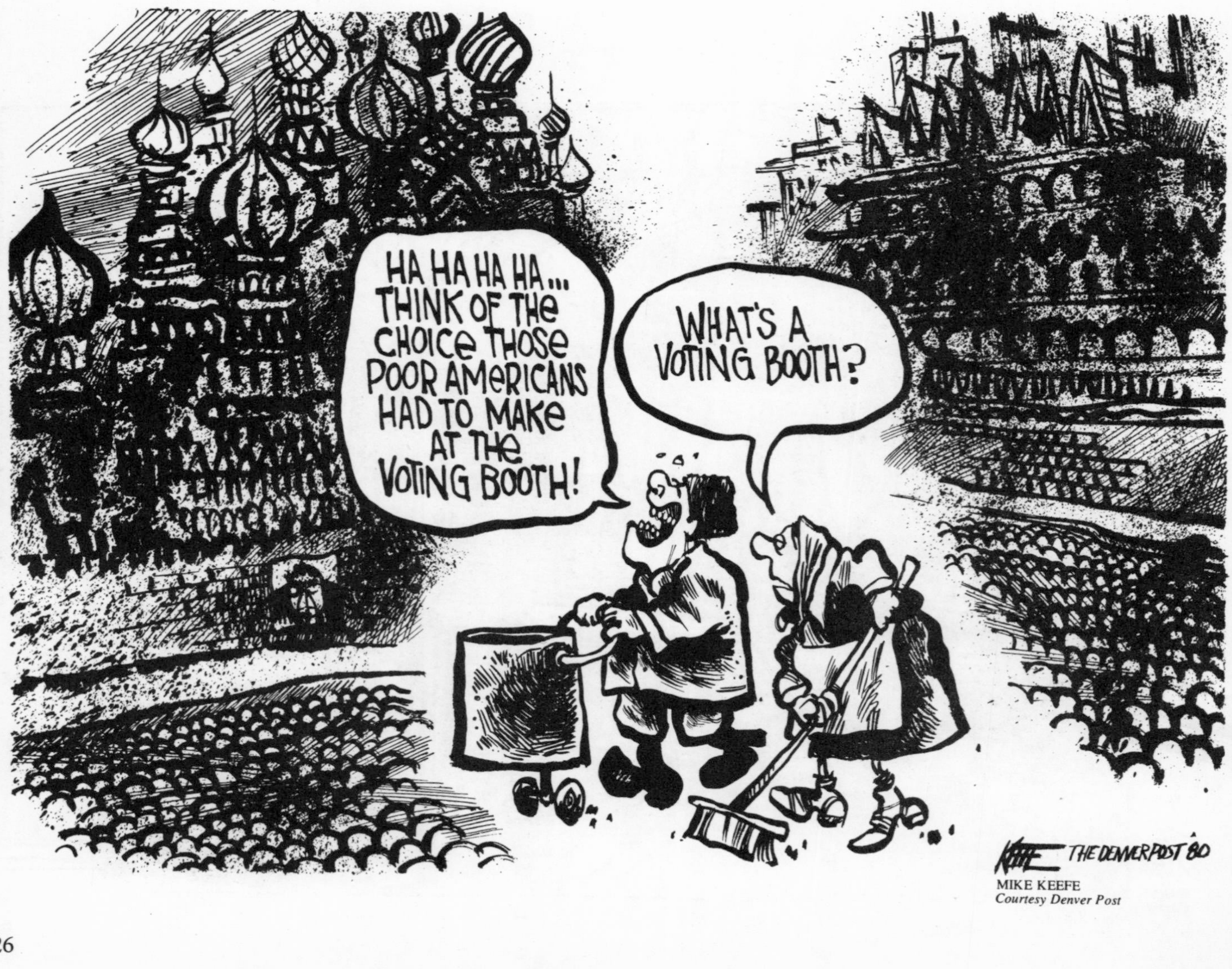
HA HA HA HA... THINK OF THE CHOICE THOSE POOR AMERICANS HAD TO MAKE AT THE VOTING BOOTH!
WHAT'S A VOTING BOOTH?
KEEFE THE DENVER POST '80

MIKE KEEFE
Courtesy Denver Post

Poland

Polish workers in scattered factories around the country walked off their jobs on July 2. They were striking for the right to form free trade unions and to protest high meat prices that had been announced the day before. Over the next few weeks more than 150 strikes took place, including one in which a railroad station was blockaded by unhappy rail workers. About 14,000 shipyard workers walked off their jobs in August and were quickly followed by another 150,000 industrial workers.

Electrician Lech Walesa organized the shipyard workers and, with other labor leaders, issued 23 demands to the Communist-controlled government. Included among the demands were the right to strike, the establishment of trade unions independent of government and Communist Party control, curbs on censorship, release of leaders jailed in previous strikes and food riots, and other social and economic improvements.

On August 30 an agreement was reached giving the workers most of what they had demanded. At the year's end, however, it was still far from clear whether the Russians would actually allow the pledges made by the Polish Communist government to be kept.

FRANK EVERS
Courtesy N. Y. Daily News

EDD ULUSCHAK
Courtesy Edmonton Journal

MIKE GRASTON
Courtesy Windsor Star

Karl Marxman

GUERNSEY LEPELLEY
Courtesy Christian Science Monitor

THE WORD THAT CANNOT BE ABIDED

CHARLES BROOKS
Courtesy Birmingham (Ala.) News

'Heard any good Polish jokes lately?'

ERIC SMITH
Courtesy Capital-Gazette (Md.) Newspapers

Nobody's Laughing

REG MANNING
Courtesy Arizona Republic

ETTA HULME
Courtesy Ft. Worth Star-Telegram

TOM CURTIS
Courtesy Milwaukee Sentinel

JACK McLEOD
Courtesy Buffalo Evening News

JEFF MACNELLY
Richmond News Leader
©Chicago Tribune—New York
    News Syndicate

Billy Carter

During much of the first three years of Jimmy Carter's term in the White House, his brother Billy had been regarded as a beer-guzzling good ole boy who liked his fun and whose antics offered amusement to the country. This image began to change, however, as he became more closely associated with an avowed enemy of the U.S.—oil-rich Libya. America's relations with Libya have been strained for years as a result of the latter's support of anti-Israeli terrorists. During the summer it was disclosed that Billy Carter had received $220,000 from the Libyan government and had registered as a foreign agent. He also had acted as an intermediary between that government and the White House.

An uproar was heard across the country questioning the propriety of such actions by the brother of the president of the United States. A special Senate subcommittee investigated the matter and determined that neither had acted illegally. The subcommittee did conclude, however, that brother Billy "merits severe criticism" for conduct "contrary to the interests of the president." It further found that President Carter had displayed poor judgment in not disassociating himself from his brother's dealings with Libya and in using Billy as a diplomat.

The affair came to be known as Billygate.

BILL GARNER
Courtesy The Commercial Appeal

JAMES LARRICK
Courtesy Clarion-Ledger,
Jackson, Miss.

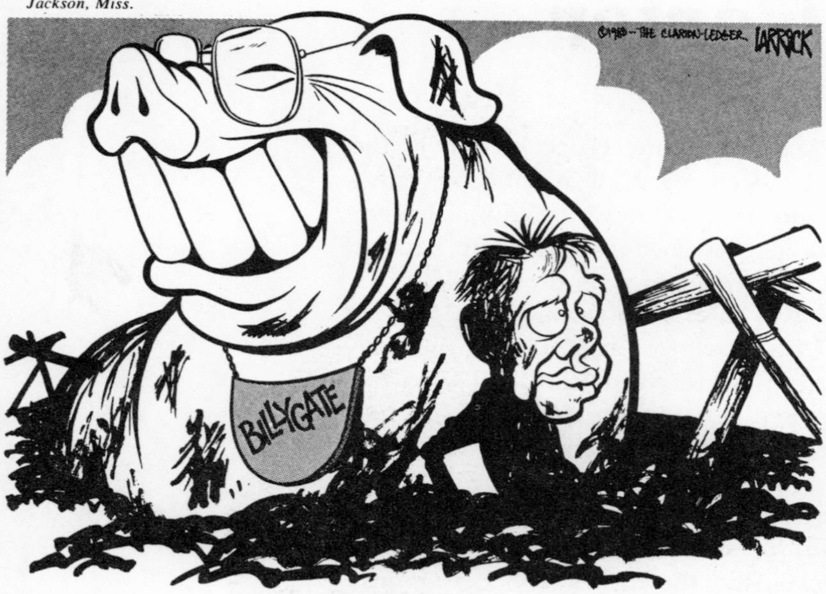
©1980—THE CLARION-LEDGER
LARRICK
BILLYGATE

"YECCHH!!"

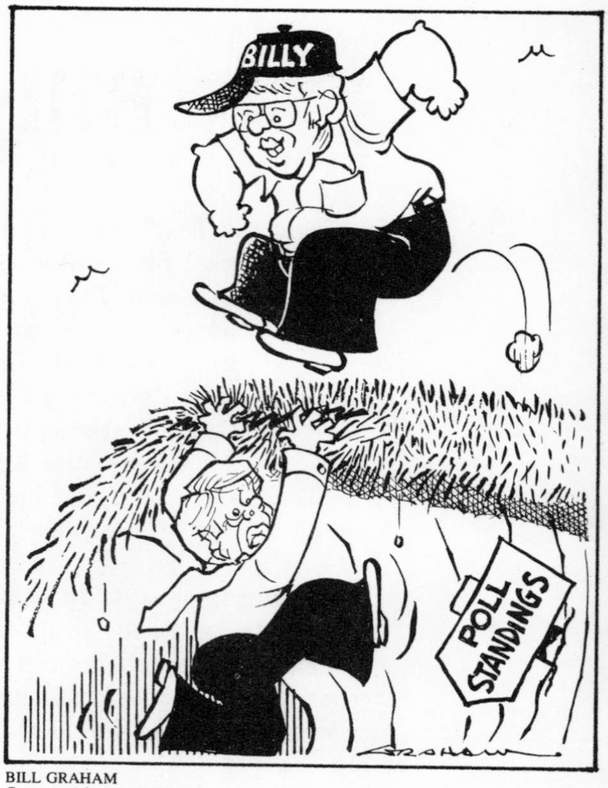
BILLY
POLL STANDINGS
GRAHAM

BILL GRAHAM
Courtesy Arkansas Gazette

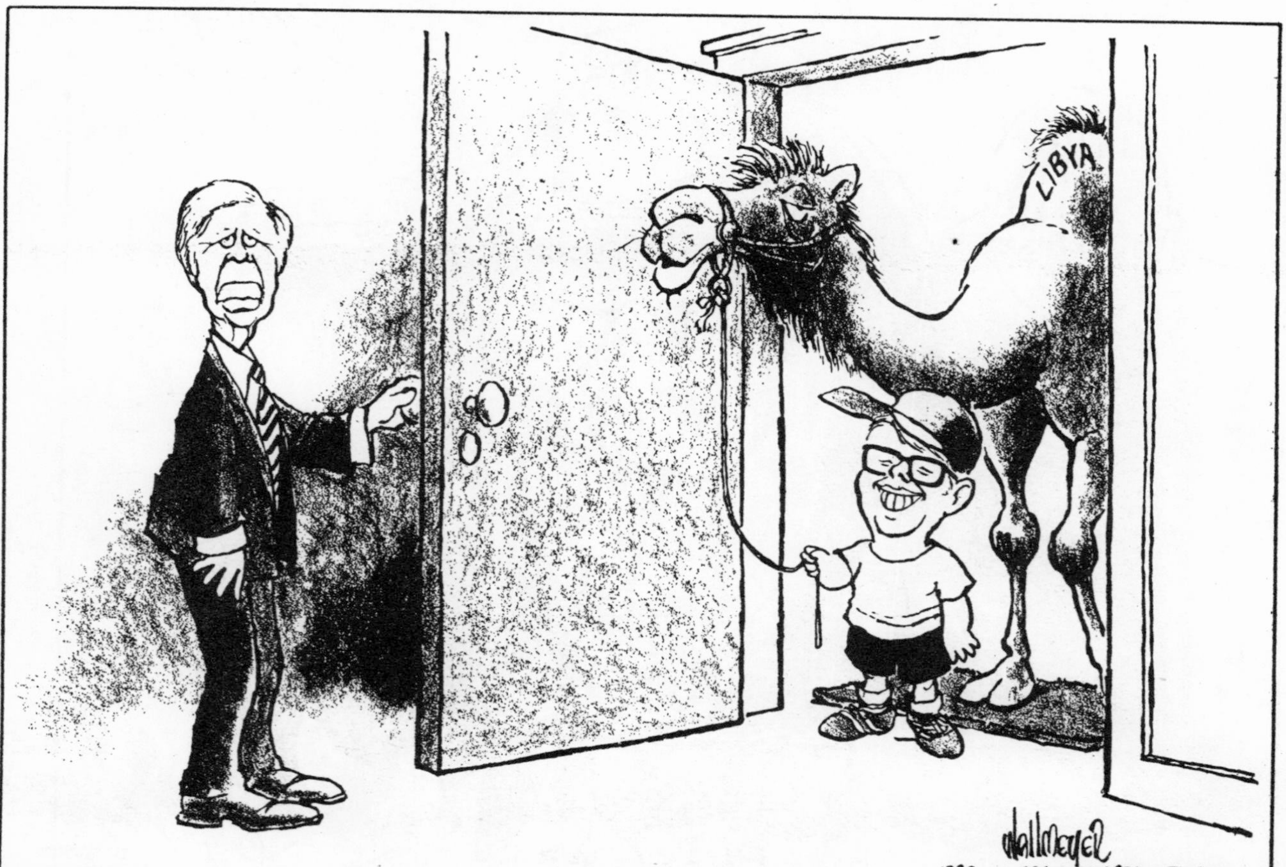
LIBYA
WALLMEYER
1980, INDEPENDENT, PRESS-TELEGRAM

DICK WALLMEYER
Long Beach Press-Telegram
©Register and Tribune Syndicate

ROB LAWLOR
Courtesy Philadelphia Daily News

BILLY GOAT

ED FISCHER
Courtesy Omaha World-Herald

BRIAN BASSET
Courtesy Seattle Times

DOUGLAS BORGSTEDT
Courtesy Philadelphia Daily News

KARL HUBENTHAL
*Courtesy Los Angeles
Herald-Examiner*

HY ROSEN
Courtesy Albany Times-Union

BILL DE ORE
Courtesy Dallas Morning News

Alice In Libyaland

-PLETCHER-
ELDON PLETCHER
New Orleans Times-Picayune
©Rothco

"...HAM...SEE WHAT BILLY'S UP TO NOW!..."

Cuba

Ever since Fidel Castro came to power, Cuban citizens have attempted to flee their country. In 1980 Castro finally gave the go-ahead for his fellow countrymen to leave in large numbers, and that is precisely what they did.

On April 1, a bus carrying Cubans wishing to emigrate broke through the gates of the Peruvian embassy in Havana. A Cuban guard was killed and Cuban security personnel were removed from the mission. After the guards left, more than 10,000 Cubans rushed to the compound seeking diplomatic asylum.

Castro was embarrassed, but managed to turn the situation around and put the Carter Administration on the spot as more and more disgruntled Cubans were allowed to leave the island. Most of them headed for the United States, which had difficulty handling the flood of immigrants.

A "freedom flotilla" of small boats shuttled back and forth between Florida and Cuba transporting the human cargo. Many of the 125,000 who sought freedom in America were convicted criminals whom Castro was delighted to dump on Uncle Sam.

DICK LOCHER
Chicago Tribune
©Chicago Tribune—N.Y.
News Syndicate

GENE BASSET
Courtesy Scripps-Howard Newspapers

BOB ARTLEY
Courtesy Worthington (Minn.) Daily Globe

BILL GARNER
Courtesy The Commercial Appeal

ECLIPSED

JOHN KNUDSEN
Courtesy N.Y. Catholic News

ED STEIN
Courtesy Rocky Mountain
News

BERT WHITMAN
Courtesy Phoenix Gazette

JAMES MORGAN
Courtesy Spartanburg Herald-Journal

'SOON YOU WILL HAVE NO ONE TO **OPPRESS**, COMRADE'

EUGENE CRAIG
Courtesy Columbus (O.) Dispatch

The Olympics

On January 20, 1980, following the Soviet Union's invasion of Afghanistan several weeks earlier, President Carter called upon the International Olympic Committee to postpone, cancel, or move the summer Olympic Games, which were scheduled for Moscow. Carter declared that the IOC should act unless the Russian troops were removed within one month.

The deadline passed without action on the part of the Soviet Union, so Carter issued a call for individual nations to boycott the summer games. Ultimately, of the 147 nations eligible to compete, only 80 took part. The U.S. Olympic Committee, under heavy pressure from Carter, kept American athletes home.

With the strongest Western competitors absent, the affair turned out to be a showcase of Soviet athletic prowess. The Russians won 80 gold medals, while their fellow ideologues, the East Germans, won 47.

BLAINE
Courtesy The Spectator, Canada

SOVIET 'OLYMPICS'

ED FISCHER
Courtesy Omaha World-Herald

CHARLES BISSELL
Courtesy The Tennessean

Bearer of the Torch and Sword

ART HENRIKSON
©Paddock Publications

MOSCOW OLYMPICS

WAR CRIMES AGAINST AFGHAN CIVILIANS

CHARLES WERNER
Courtesy Indianapolis Star

ANDY DONATO
Courtesy Toronto Sun

ERIC SMITH
Courtesy Capital-Gazette (Md.) Newspapers

143

GEORGE FISHER
Courtesy Arkansas Gazette

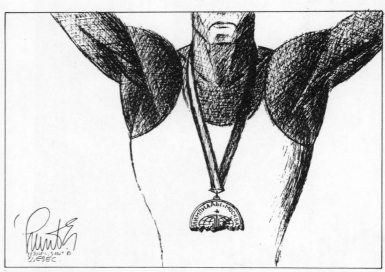

RAOUL HUNTER
Courtesy Le Soleil (Quebec)

JR THORNTON
JAN 80

JOHN R. THORNTON
*Courtesy Republican Journal
(Belfast, Me.)*

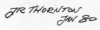

ANTHONY JENKINS
Courtesy Toronto Globe and Mail

CRAIG MACINTOSH
Courtesy Minneapolis Star

OLYMPIC COVERAGE

HEAR NO EVIL · SEE NO EVIL · SPEAK NO EVIL

CHUCK AYERS
CHUCK AYERS
Courtesy Akron Beacon Journal

SANDY CAMPBELL
Courtesy The Tennessean

SIBERIA

MIKE GRASTON
Courtesy Windsor Star

. . . And Other Issues

JERRY FEARING
Courtesy St. Paul Dispatch

CHARLES DANIEL
Courtesy Knoxville Journal

LARRY WRIGHT
Courtesy Detroit News

JACK BENDER
Waterloo Courier
©Rothco Cartoons, Inc.

RICHARD CROWSON
Courtesy Jackson (Tenn.) Sun

News Item: President of the Southern
Baptist Convention said, "Almighty God does
not hear the prayer of a Jew."

GEORGE FISHER
Courtesy Arkansas Gazette

VIC RUNTZ
Courtesy Bangor Daily News

MIKE KEEFE
Courtesy Denver Post

BILL GARNER
Courtesy The Commercial Appeal

AL LIEDERMAN
Courtesy Long Island Press

JIM BERRY
©NEA

RAY OSRIN
Courtesy Cleveland Plain Dealer

JOHN BRANCH
Courtesy Chapel Hill News

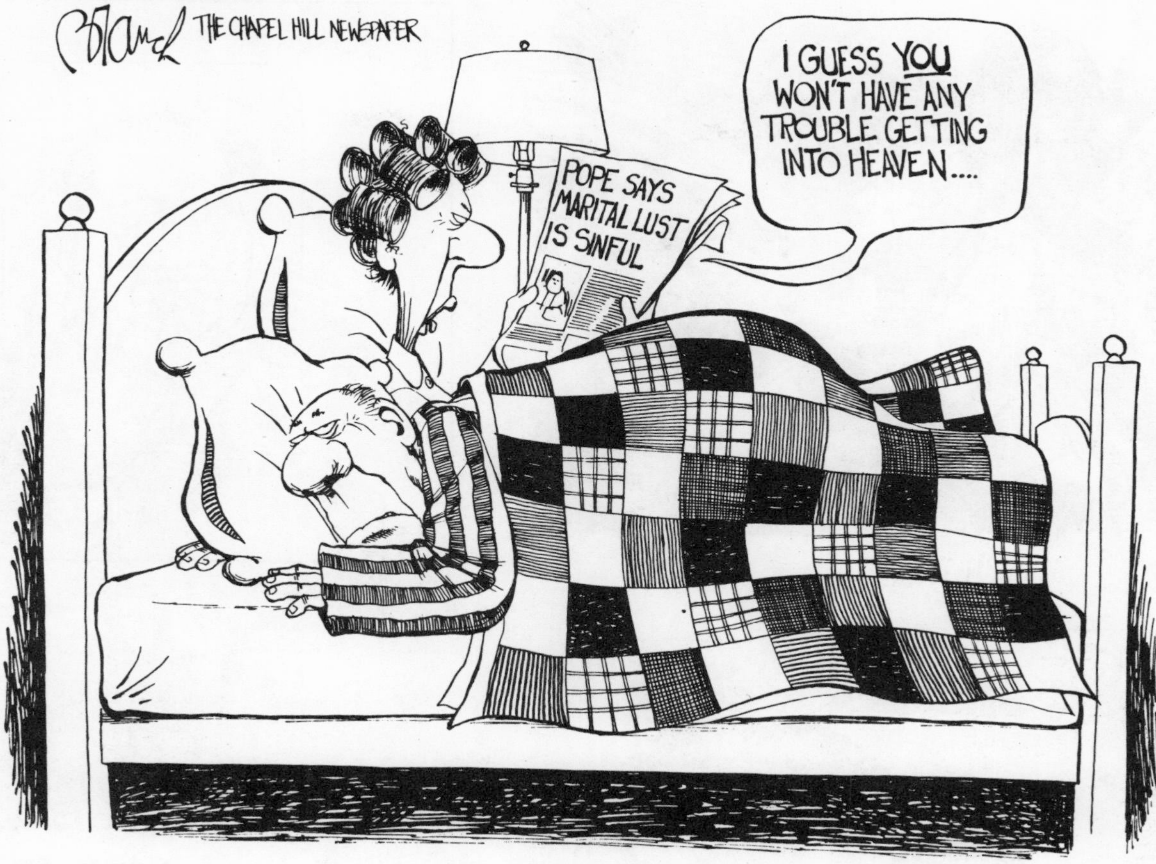
THE CHAPEL HILL NEWSPAPER
I GUESS YOU WON'T HAVE ANY TROUBLE GETTING INTO HEAVEN....
POPE SAYS MARITAL LUST IS SINFUL

JIM BORGMAN
Courtesy Cincinnati Enquirer

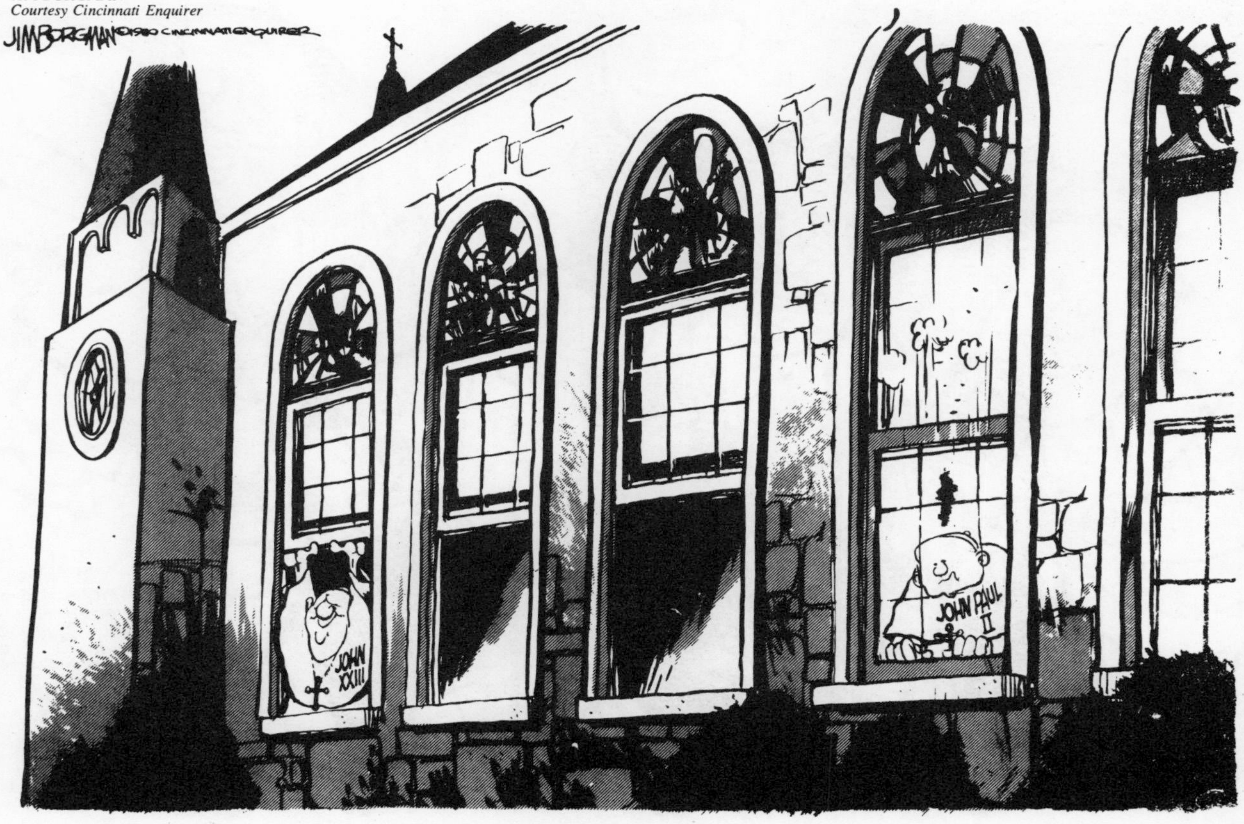
JIM BORGMAN
JOHN XXIII
JOHN PAUL II

PATRICK CROWLEY
Courtesy West Palm Beach Post

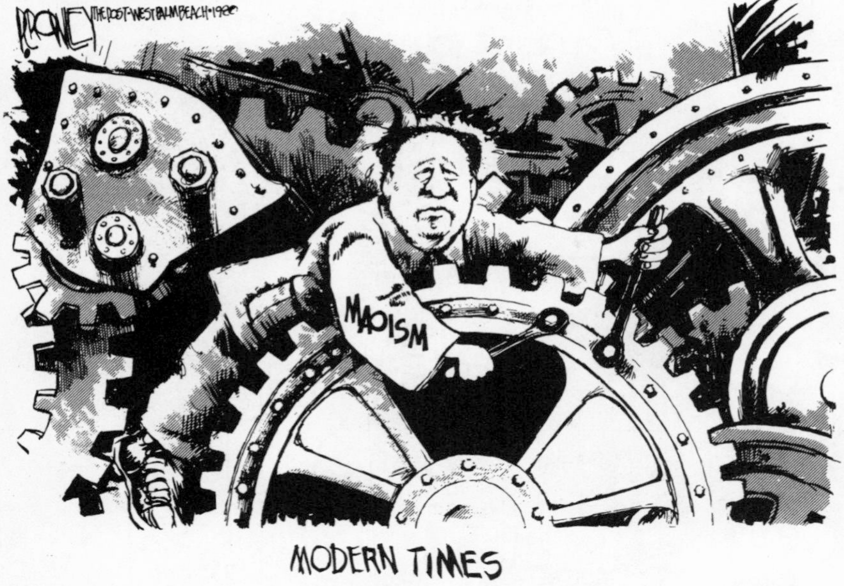
THE POST-WEST PALM BEACH 1980
MAOISM
MODERN TIMES

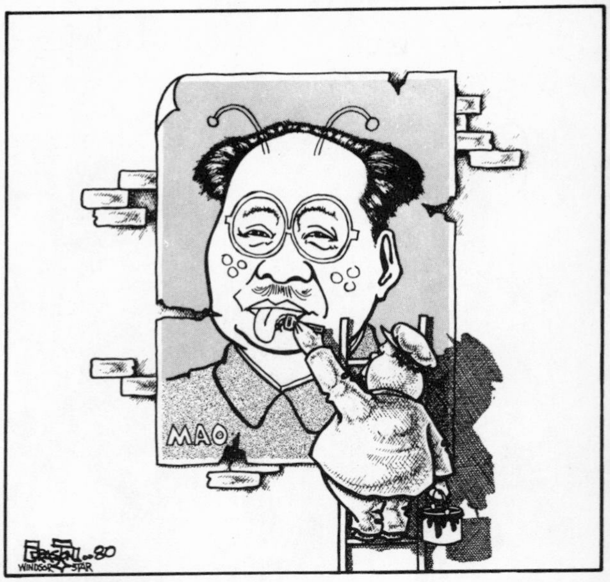
MAO
WINDSOR STAR

MIKE GRASTON
Courtesy Windsor Star

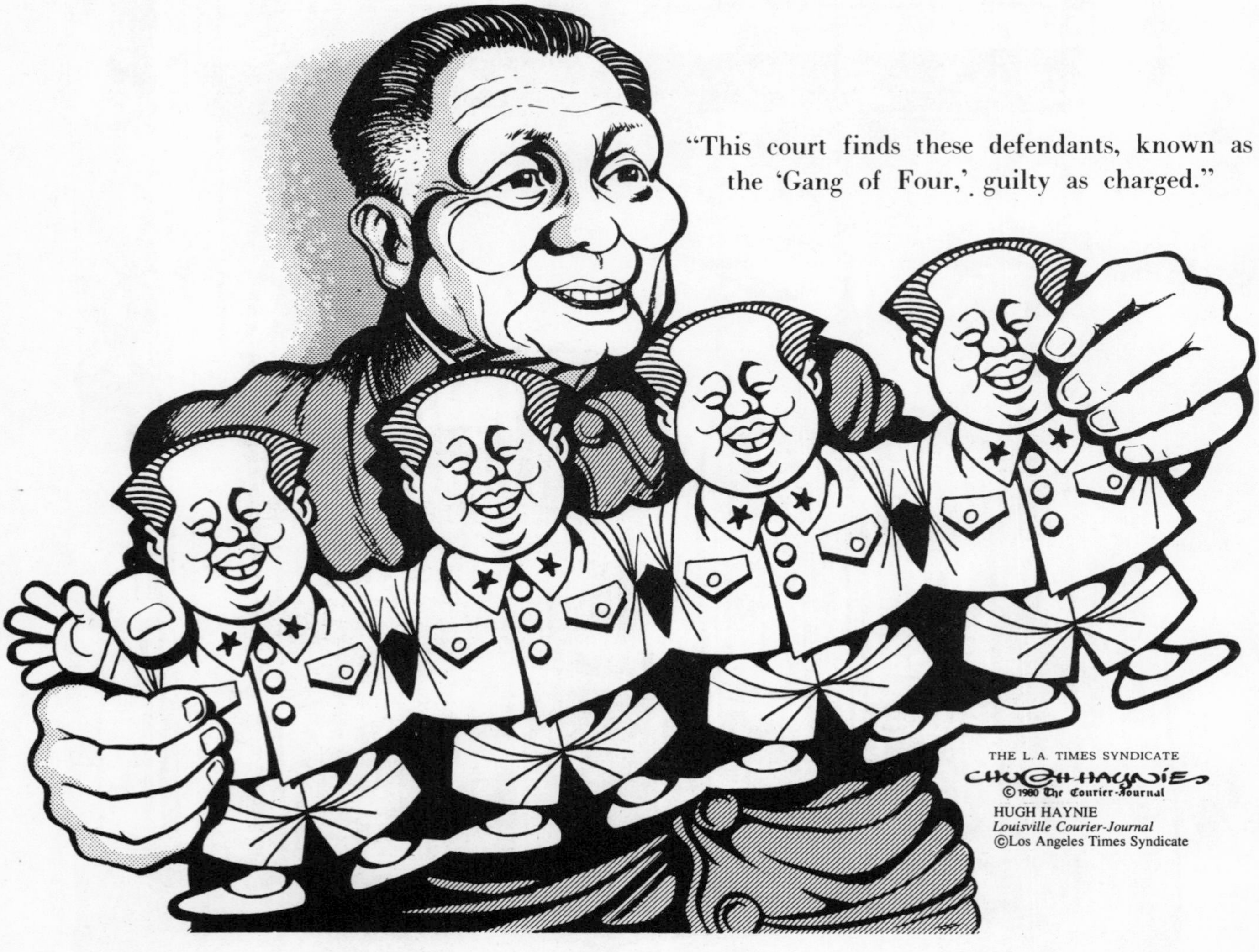
THE L. A. TIMES SYNDICATE
HUGH HAYNIE
© 1980 The Courier-Journal

"This court finds these defendants, known as the 'Gang of Four,' guilty as charged."

HUGH HAYNIE
Louisville Courier-Journal

CHAN LOWE
Courtesy Oklahoma City Times

SANDY CAMPBELL
Courtesy The Tennessean

PAUL DUGINSKI
Courtesy Sacramento Union

DAVE GRANLUND
Courtesy Middlesex News

PHIL BISSELL
Courtesy Salem (Mass.)
Evening News

THE BIG SQUEEZE...APRIL 15TH

BOB ENGLEHART
Courtesy Dayton Journal Herald

"I THINK YOU WANT THE ATHLETIC CLUB NEXT DOOR. WE'RE SIXTIES RADICALS!"

JERRY ROBINSON
©Cartoonists and Writers
Snydicate

JOHN TREVER
*Courtesy Albuquerque
Journal*

JIMMY JOHNSON
Courtesy Jackson (Miss.)
Daily News

BOB ALEXANDER
Courtesy Lawrence (Mass.) Eagle-Tribune

ROB LAWLOR
Courtesy Philadelphia Daily News

Past Award Winners

PULITZER PRIZE EDITORIAL CARTOON

1922—Rollin Kirby, New York World
1924—J. N. Darling, New York Herald Tribune
1925—Rollin Kirby, New York World
1926—D. R. Fitzpatrick, St. Louis Post-Dispatch
1927—Nelson Harding, Brooklyn Eagle
1928—Nelson Harding, Brooklyn Eagle
1929—Rollin Kirby, New York World
1930—Charles Macauley, Brooklyn Eagle
1931—Edmund Duffy, Baltimore Sun
1932—John T. McCutcheon, Chicago Tribune
1933—H. M. Talburt, Washington Daily News
1934—Edmund Duffy, Baltimore Sun
1935—Ross A. Lewis, Milwaukee Journal
1937—C. D. Batchelor, New York Daily News
1938—Vaughn Shoemaker, Chicago Daily News
1939—Charles G. Werner, Daily Oklahoman
1940—Edmund Duffy, Baltimore Sun
1941—Jacob Burck, Chicago Times
1942—Herbert L. Block, Newspaper Enterprise Association
1943—Jay N. Darling, New York Herald Tribune
1944—Clifford K. Berryman, Washington Star
1945—Bill Mauldin, United Feature Syndicate
1946—Bruce Russell, Los Angeles Times
1947—Vaughn Shoemaker, Chicago Daily News
1948—Reuben L. (Rube) Goldberg, New York Sun
1949—Lute Pease, Newark Evening News
1950—James T. Berryman, Washington Star
1951—Reginald W. Manning, Arizona Republic
1952—Fred L. Packer, New York Mirror
1953—Edward D. Kuekes, Cleveland Plain Dealer
1954—Herbert L. Block, Washington Post
1955—Daniel R. Fitzpatrick, St. Louis Post-Dispatch
1956—Robert York, Louisville Times
1957—Tom Little, Nashville Tennessean
1958—Bruce M. Shanks, Buffalo Evening News
1959—Bill Mauldin, St. Louis Post-Dispatch
1961—Carey Orr, Chicago Tribune
1962—Edmund S. Valtman, Hartford Times
1963—Frank Miller, Des Moines Register
1964—Paul Conrad, Denver Post
1966—Don Wright, Miami News
1967—Patrick B. Oliphant, Denver Post
1968—Eugene Gray Payne, Charlotte Observer
1969—John Fischetti, Chicago Daily News
1970—Thomas F. Darcy, Newsday
1971—Paul Conrad, Los Angeles Times
1972—Jeffrey K. MacNelly, Richmond News Leader
1974—Paul Szep, Boston Globe
1975—Garry Trudeau, Universal Press Syndicate

1976—Tony Auth, Philadelphia Enquirer
1977—Paul Szep, Boston Globe
1978—Jeff MacNelly, Richmond News Leader
1979—Herbert Block, Washington Post
1980—Don Wright, Miami News

NOTE: Pulitzer Prize Award was not given 1923, 1936, 1960, 1965, and 1973.

SIGMA DELTA CHI AWARD EDITORIAL CARTOON

1942—Jacob Burck, Chicago Times
1943—Charles Werner, Chicago Sun
1944—Henry Barrow, Associated Press
1945—Reuben L. Goldberg, New York Sun
1946—Dorman H. Smith, Newspaper Enterprise Association
1947—Bruce Russell, Los Angeles Times
1948—Herbert Block, Washington Post
1949—Herbert Block, Washington Post
1950—Bruce Russell, Los Angeles Times
1951—Herbert Block, Washington Post, and
        Bruce Russell, Los Angeles Times
1952—Cecil Jensen, Chicago Daily News
1953—John Fischetti, Newspaper Enterprise Association
1954—Calvin Alley, Memphis Commercial Appeal
1955—John Fischetti, Newspaper Enterprise Association
1956—Herbert Block, Washington Post
1957—Scott Long, Minneapolis Tribune
1958—Clifford H. Baldowski, Atlanta Constitution
1959—Charles G. Brooks, Birmingham News
1960—Dan Dowling, New York Herald-Tribune
1961—Frank Interlandi, Des Moines Register
1962—Paul Conrad, Denver Post
1963—William Mauldin, Chicago Sun-Times
1964—Charles Bissell, Nashville Tennessean
1965—Roy Justus, Minneapolis Star
1966—Patrick Oliphant, Denver Post
1967—Eugene Payne, Charlotte Observer
1968—Paul Conrad, Los Angeles Times
1969—William Mauldin, Chicago Sun-Times
1970—Paul Conrad, Los Angeles Times
1971—Hugh Haynie, Louisville Courier-Journal
1972—William Mauldin, Chicago Sun-Times
1973—Paul Szep, Boston Globe
1974—Mike Peters, Dayton Daily News
1975—Tony Auth, Philadelphia Enquirer
1976—Paul Szep, Boston Globe
1977—Don Wright, Miami News
1978—Jim Borgman, Cincinnati Enquirer
1979—John P. Trever, Albuquerque Journal

NATIONAL HEADLINERS CLUB AWARD EDITORIAL CARTOON

1938—C. D. Batchelor, New York Daily News
1939—John Knott, Dallas News
1940—Herbert Block, Newspaper Enterprise Association
1941—Charles H. Sykes, Philadelphia Evening Ledger
1942—Jerry Doyle, Philadelphia Record
1943—Vaughn Shoemaker, Chicago Daily News
1944—Roy Justus, Sioux City Journal
1945—F. O. Alexander, Philadelphia Bulletin
1946—Hank Barrow, Associated Press
1947—Cy Hungerford, Pittsburgh Post-Gazette
1948—Tom Little, Nashville Tennessean
1949—Bruce Russell, Los Angeles Times
1950—Dorman Smith, Newspaper Enterprise Association
1951—C. G. Werner, Indianapolis Star
1952—John Fischetti, Newspaper Enterprise Association
1953—James T. Berryman and Gib Crockett, Washington Star
1954—Scott Long, Minneapolis Tribune
1955—Leo Thiele, Los Angeles Mirror-News
1956—John Milt Morris, Associated Press
1957—Frank Miller, Des Moines Register
1958—Burris Jenkins, Jr., New York Journal-American
1959—Karl Hubenthal, Los Angeles Examiner
1960—Don Hesse, St. Louis Globe-Democrat
1961—L. D. Warren, Cincinnati Enquirer
1962—Franklin Morse, Los Angeles Mirror
1963—Charles Bissell, Nashville Tennessean
1964—Lou Grant, Oakland Tribune
1965—Merle R. Tingley, London (Ont.) Free Press
1966—Hugh Haynie, Louisville Courier-Journal
1967—Jim Berry, Newspaper Enterprise Association
1968—Warren King, New York News
1969—Larry Barton, Toledo Blade
1970—Bill Crawford, Newspaper Enterprise Association
1971—Ray Osrin, Cleveland Plain Dealer
1972—Jacob Burck, Chicago Sun-Times
1973—Ranan Lurie, New York Times
1974—Tom Darcy, Newsday
1975—Bill Sanders, Milwaukee Journal
1976—No award given
1977—Paul Szep, Boston Globe
1978—Dwane Powell, Raleigh News and Observer
1979—Pat Oliphant, Washington Star
1980—Don Wright, Miami News

NATIONAL NEWSPAPER AWARD / CANADA EDITORIAL CARTOON

1949—Jack Boothe, Toronto Globe and Mail
1950—James G. Reidford, Montreal Star
1951—Len Norris, Vancouver Sun
1952—Robert La Palme, Le Devoir, Montreal
1953—Robert W. Chambers, Halifax Chronicle-Herald
1954—John Collins, Montreal Gazette
1955—Merle R. Tingley, London Free Press
1956—James G. Reidford, Toronto Globe and Mail
1957—James G. Reidford, Toronto Globe and Mail
1958—Raoul Hunter, Le Soleil, Quebec
1959—Duncan Macpherson, Toronto Star
1960—Duncan Macpherson, Toronto Star
1961—Ed McNally, Montreal Star
1962—Duncan Macpherson, Toronto Star
1963—Jan Kamienski, Winnipeg Tribune
1964—Ed McNally, Montreal Star
1965—Duncan Macpherson, Toronto Star
1966—Robert W. Chambers, Halifax Chronicle-Herald
1967—Raoul Hunter, Le Soleil, Quebec
1968—Roy Peterson, Vancouver Sun
1969—Edward Uluschak, Edmonton Journal
1970—Duncan Macpherson, Toronto Daily Star
1971—Yardley Jones, Toronto Sun
1972—Duncan Macpherson, Toronto Star
1973—John Collins, Montreal Gazette
1974—Blaine, Hamilton Spectator
1975—Roy Peterson, Vancouver Sun
1976—Andy Donato, Toronto Sun
1977—Terry Mosher, Montreal Gazette
1978—Terry Mosher, Montreal Gazette
1979—Edd Uluschak, Edmonton Journal

Index

INDEX